Passion

Mar
Mab

&

Miles Franklin

by
Sylvia Martin

ONLYWOMEN PRESS LTD
London

Published in 2001 by Onlywomen Press Limited, London, UK.

ISBN 0 906500 64 8

BRITISH LIBRARY CATALOGUING-IN-PUBLICATION DATA
A catalogue record for this book is available from the British Library.

designed and typeset by Andrew Lindesay
cover design: Spark
Printed and bound in the United Kingdom by Mackays of Chatham plc.

ACKNOWLEDGEMENTS

PROLOGUE   5

1   The Women Behind the Words   9

2   Mary   18

3   Mabel and Miles   31

4   Suffragists and Pacifists   40

5   Poetry and Desire   55

6   A Child is Born   64

7   To England and Back   74

8   'I to the Guard Belong'   85

9   England: New Beginnings   99

10 Meeting Miles   110

11 The Chastity Knot   118

12 181c High Street, Kensington   131

13 Secrets   144

14 'An Exhilaration of Tragedy'   159

15 Postscript   172

    NOTES   180

    BIBLIOGRAPHY   187

This book is based on research done for a Ph.D. thesis at Griffith University, Brisbane, Australia, for which I received the assistance of a Griffith University Postgraduate Award. Kay Ferres supervised that thesis and I owe her a special debt of thanks. The project was further assisted by the Commonwealth Government through the Australia Council, its arts funding and advisory body.

Denis Singleton, the late Eileen Singleton and their daughter, Valerie Singleton, provided invaluable assistance with their personal memories of Mabel Singleton, Mary Fullerton and Miles Franklin. Wing Commander D.G. Singleton OBE also generously allowed photographs from his personal collection to be reproduced. I would like to thank Mary Fullerton's nephew, Oliver Jenks, for permission to quote from her papers held in Australian libraries. The State Library of New South Wales gave permission to quote from the Miles Franklin Papers held in the Mitchell Library. I would like to thank the librarians from the State Library of New South Wales (in particular, Jennifer Broomhead), The National Library of Australia, the State Library of Victoria, and Griffith University Library for their assistance.

I am grateful to Jenny Lee and Pearlie McNeill who read and commented on an earlier draft. My thanks go also to Lilian Mohin for her final editing of the manuscript. I am personally indebted to the friends and colleagues who have assisted me throughout the writing of this book by making research material available, suggesting avenues to follow, and supporting me with their interest in and enthusiasm for the project. I would particularly like to thank Matthew Stephens, James Renwick, Shelagh Doyle, Colleen Burke, Joy Hooton, Jill Roe, Andrea Weiss, Ros Mills, Margaret Somerville, Laura Hartley, Sari Wawn, Sophie Cunningham and Astrid Stephens. Lizzie Mulder has my very special thanks. This book is also for her.

Recently in London I stood in front of 181 High Street Kensington, Mary Fullerton and Mabel Singleton's address in the 1930s. Miles Franklin stayed with them there for over a year when she visited London in 1931. Flat C in this elegant Edwardian building now houses a firm of solicitors. The pizza joint and gas showroom on either side of the entrance are obvious newcomers, but the sullen stone cherub above the door leading to the floors above would have glowered down on the women who passed in and out of it all those years ago. From my vantage point on the pavement opposite, I imagined I could see the outline of a woman's head at one of the upper windows. What might it have been like inside that room then?

A woman sits by the window, tapping the keys of a portable typewriter. The light falling on her short grey hair momentarily silvers it. Her profile is sharp. Hair combed back from a high forehead, jutting cheekbone, straight nose, thin mouth. A face that in its spareness shows everything yet reveals nothing. The eyes are hidden. She stops typing, removes the page from the typewriter, and reads aloud what she has written:

> *Seven Thirty a.m.*
> *The mad woman is passing down the street,*
> *Shouting foolishness*
> *As she does every morning*
> *While I eat my early toast,*
> *Drink my cup of tea,*
> *And open my paper*
> *Beginning my decorous day . . .*
> *I put up a prayer:*
> *Oh good Grey Matter*
> *Guardian of dignity,*
> *Be true, stand true.*[1]

Her slightly flattened vowels betray Australian origins, though she is sitting in a large, airy living room two floors above High Street Kensington, London. It is now 8.30 and the mad woman's early

5

morning cries have given way to blaring horns and screeching brakes, the sounds of a city bustling towards another working day. But here those sounds are muffled. The woman dips a pen in the pot of black ink that stands beside the typewriter and signs the poem with her name – Mary E. Fullerton – in a flowing hand that is a surprising contrast to the angular planes of her face. A flourish on the 'n' and then the date, 1st September, 1934.

Footsteps mount the wooden staircase that can be seen through the open doorway and the poet raises her head, revealing startlingly blue eyes. Her face softens as she greets the woman who strides in, cheeks pink and glowing from the cold morning air. This woman looks younger than the seated poet, full-figured where Mary is thin to the point of gauntness. Her presence fills the room.

This is Mabel Singleton. Mary had met the young English-woman in Melbourne in 1909 when they were both active in the Women's Political Association, campaigning for suffragist Vida Goldstein in her bid to become the first woman in federal parliament. It is not difficult to imagine Mabel haranguing the crowds that gathered on the Yarra Bank, at the place known as the Trafalgar Square of the Antipodes. Just as the mob jeered at the members of the so-called shrieking sisterhood who spoke out for women's rights in the London square, so Mabel and Mary were heckled by the crowds that flocked to the Melbourne river bank. Mabel found the challenge exhilarating and she was a persuasive speaker; she enjoyed the thrill of battle. Charm was a natural gift that she had learned to use well. Mary preferred speaking at the WPA's regular 'At Home' gatherings, where her quiet wit and literary talents were appreciated. Her shyness made every political public address a terrifying challenge to overcome, though her audience would not have suspected it. This woman's strength was tenacity.

'How was your walk?' Mary leans back against the comfortable bosom of her friend, who now stands at the desk by the window, one arm lightly encircling the older woman's shoulders.

'Bracing, to say the least.' Mabel massages Mary's shoulder. 'A squirrel scampered right up to me in the Gardens – Miles would

have loved it.' She reminds her friend how Miles Franklin used to fill her pockets with bread to feed the squirrels when they went walking, how she'd once taken out her handkerchief at a literary afternoon tea at Henry Handel Richardson's and showered crumbs onto the Persian rug. 'She probably made it worse by chuckling like a kookaburra.'

The women smile at the memory of the Australian writer who had visited in 1931 and stayed at 181c High Street for over a year. Miles Franklin was not unlike a squirrel herself with her darting movements, her always watchful eyes, her unstoppable energy. But sometimes she'd retire to her room for hours, occasionally even days at a time without warning, as if retreating out of reach, to the high branches of an oak tree.

Mary is brought back to the present sharply as Mabel picks up the page lying on the desk beside the battered portable.

'What's this? A new poem?'

'Nothing much.' The poet tries to reclaim it but her friend quickly moves out of reach, glances over the piece, then kisses the top of Mary's head.

'You've got more "grey matter" than anyone I know, my dear. And it's not all visible. Now I must get downstairs to the office.' She whisks the breakfast tray off the desk and is gone.

Mary stares out of the window for a few moments but her eyes do not take in the rooftops opposite with their forest of chimneys outlined against an almost colourless sky. What she sees are the grey-green eucalypts of the Gippsland bush, the memory of whose summer scent can still make her mouth dry with longing. Today, September 1st, is the beginning of spring there. September is a month of great significance for Mary: it was the month she met Mabel in Melbourne on the campaign trail, Mabel's birthday too. In a birthday poem Mary wrote for her in 1910, spring, September and new love are intertwined:

> 'Twas last September – in Australia's Spring –
> But almost in my heart the Autumn time;
> Its Spring seemed flown, its Summer withering;
> Thou cam'st and set the bells again a-chime,
> And made my heart September . . . [2]

Mary sighs as she adds her latest poem to the pile in the desk drawer, then inserts a fresh sheet of paper into the typewriter. Her eyes are not sad, however; she has found a different sense of home in London. She has maintained the threads binding her to Australia through her letters to her sisters in Melbourne, but she is especially nourished by her friendship with Miles Franklin, who understands those bonds more than anyone else. Her fingers move swiftly over the keys:

Dear Many Miles Away ...

THE WOMEN BEHIND THE WORDS

' I only wish for means to be a recluse and get away from everyone and what they say, and don't care if I'm never mentioned after my death. I don't want the scavengers and malicious muck-rakers romancing to show off their talents at my expense', wrote Miles Franklin to Mary Fullerton in 1930.[1] At the risk of being labelled a scavenger (or worse), I must at the outset declare that I love delving into library archives. My particular passion is exploring the papers of women who led unorthodox lives, who did not marry or who sustained significant friendships with other women. Deciphering impossible handwriting, attempting to make sense of incomplete letters, trying to fit undated letters into a time scheme, identifying people listed casually in diaries by a first name or even an initial – these are some of the pleasures and frustrations involved in such a project. Sometimes the detective trail leads to other library collections across the country, even overseas as in my research for this book. Knowing that, unlike a detective novel, the story can never be complete, case solved, ends tied up neatly, part of the intrigue lies in the very fragmentary nature of the exercise; like life itself, these lives are all the more intriguing for their gaps and silences.

My interest in the little-known Australian writer, Mary Fullerton, began when I dipped into the large correspondence left to the Mitchell Library in Sydney by her more famous colleague, Miles Franklin. That writer's first book, *My Brilliant Career*, is still read avidly by young women in Australia almost a century after it was first published, and Gillian Armstrong's 1979 film has added another dimension to this feminist classic. Miles was also a prolific letter writer who kept copies of her own letters and stored up the replies. There are thousands in the Mitchell and about 800 of these are between Miles Franklin and Mary Fullerton, written between 1922 and 1946 when Mary was living in England.

It's a fascinating correspondence that ranges widely: they chat about day to day activities, discuss the highs and lows of the writing process, and cook up convoluted schemes to maintain the secrecy of their pseudonyms, particularly Miles Franklin's Brent of Bin Bin persona. Analysing the position of women writers, especially those from the "colonies", is a favourite topic. Philosophising is interspersed with gossip and the letters are peppered liberally with witty and often scathing comments about fellow authors and recalcitrant publishers. Of particular interest to me is the fact that Mary Fullerton often talks about Mabel Singleton, the woman with whom she shares a series of flats throughout the years in London, and Mabel's son, Denis, whom they seem to have brought up together. I found that Miles Franklin had kept correspondence between herself and Mabel Singleton too, right up to 1952. I was hooked.

From the Miles Franklin Papers I turned to the Mary Fullerton Papers, also held in the Mitchell. Mary was a most prolific writer. Best known as a poet, she had five volumes of poetry published (two under the pseudonym 'E') as well as five novels (under various names), a book of autobiographical sketches, a non-fiction book on Australia for English readers, and a curious collection of comic Australian phrases published in 1916 under the pseudonym, Turner O'Lingo. As a journalist, she published in Australian and English newspapers and magazines, under her own name and a variety of pseudonyms. Much of the writing that flowed from her pen (and trusty portable typewriter) remains unpublished and it's all neatly parcelled up in her papers in folders tied up with pink library tape.

When I met Denis Singleton and his wife in London in 1992 (sadly, my only meeting with Eileen, who died three months later), I was told what Eileen called 'a funny story' about these papers. After Mabel Singleton died in 1965, it was discovered that she still had a large number of her friend's manuscripts in her possession. They remained in a cupboard at the home of her son and daughter-in-law for several years. Eileen confessed to me that one day, in frustration at having once more to move the box containing the manuscripts in order to gain access to the cupboard, she had picked it up and put it out with the rubbish. Fortunately, after having second thoughts and ringing an acquaintance at Angus & Robertson's for advice, she retrieved the box and set in motion the process that eventually resulted in Mitchell Library's acquisition of the collection, now catalogued as the Mary Fullerton Papers.

Apart from the librarian who organised the papers and wrote the library guide to their contents, I suspect I may have been the first reader to open some of the folders crammed with loose sheets of unpublished poems, many of them carbon copies of typescript, some handwritten neatly as if for presentation, others scrawled in pencil.[2] They cover a variety of subjects and poetic forms. An "acrostic" sonnet, typed and dated 19 May 1910, first drew my attention as I turned the flimsy sheets:

> M-y thoughts weave fancies: Did the gods foresee
> A-down the track of our untrodden days
> B-eyond old hours, the meeting of our ways,
> E-re time should end, the things that were to be;
> L-ove in my heart, inspiring song from me,
> S-ong from my heart spontaneous in praise:
> I-n years of old was I designed to raise
> N-ow as I sing them, ardent songs to thee?
>
> G-ods if ye meant it not, why did ye make
> L-ong, long ago, and ere I found her here
> E-re she ever saw me; these for me to take
> T-o thread a rhyme upon, her letters clear
> O-ne for every sonnet-line – given for my sake –
> N-ame for a sonnet – and I a sonneteer?

The title of another was 'The Lips of My Love' and contained the lines:

> For the eyes of my love
>   Were her soul
> And the lips of my love were her touch
> And she made me a part of her soul.
>
> Then I knew what love is
>   And I knew that a kiss
> Means more than the pulse's brief bliss
> It means, oh my love, it means this.

I found that many of the poems had the dates on which Mary wrote them. Some were also signed, and many had dedications such as: 'Mabel', 'M.E.S from M.E.F', 'With more love than can be spoken or written', and 'To you who thought of me in absence'. Most of the poems carrying dedications to the poet's friend were written in the decade between 1910 and 1920, although some are dated as late as the 1940s.

Mary Fullerton is best remembered as a poet (in as far as she is remembered at all), and almost entirely for the short, terse, philosophical pieces that comprise the last two published volumes, *Moles Do So Little With Their Privacy* and *The Wonder and the Apple*. These poems were compared with those of Emily Dickinson when they came out in the 1940s (Dame Mary Gilmore thought the affinities were 'Emily Dickinson a little too much').[3] Described as 'universal rather than local in content', 'Security' is typical of the later poems:

> The gulls that superintend the tides,
> And love the daring foam,
> Know where stout permanence abides,
> And make the cliff their home.[4]

The hundred or so surviving poems Mary Fullerton wrote for Mabel Singleton are very different from the later published poems, in content and style. These poems are highly personal, often written for particular occasions or as an emotional response to her friend's changeable moods. They were not intended for publication, although occasionally a non-specifically gendered love poem, such as 'Dearness', also appears in print.[5] As well as dating and dedicating the unpublished poems, the poet frequently noted the location they were written, even the time of day. If they are read in the context of what is known of Mary and Mabel's lives through letters, diaries, memoirs, magazines like *Woman Voter* and Denis Singleton's personal memories, they map an unusual love story that ranges over more than thirty years and two continents. The poems also offer a wonderful opportunity to enter into the private thoughts of a woman as she struggles to conceptualise her love for her woman friend positively. She draws from a variety of theories that were current, taking up some and rejecting others as she searches for a poetic language to express her feelings.

The treatment by conventional biographers and historians of women who remain single and/or who sustain close friendships with other women follows predictable lines. They dwell on any possible liaisons with men, often employing variations of the fiancé-lost-in-the-war storyline, and friendships with women are either played down, glossed over or ignored. Even well meaning feminist biographies tend to acknowledge possible sexual elements in same-sex relationships and then to firmly shut the bedroom door on any further speculation or analysis. One can almost hear the sigh of relief. Occasionally, on the other hand, biographers show a prurient fascination about single women's sexuality and its possible "abnormality"; here the offenders are usually male.

The small amount that has been written about Mary Fullerton and the more extensive biographical material on Miles Franklin provide examples of these predictable lines. In the case of Mary Fullerton, Mabel Singleton is referred to as 'a friend' or 'a patron' and no further speculation is entered into; Mary's single state is explained by her own statement in 'Memoirs' that she was a 'go alone' woman.[6] Miles Franklin has been given the prurient treatment by one male biographer,[7] while feminists writing about her life tend to agree with Drusilla Modjeska's sympathetic but bemused assessment that she was 'a curious character . . . hard to pin down, contradictory and idiosyncratic'.[8] Miles's early relationship with her male cousin and some later liaisons during her time in America have been mulled over, but the influential and long-standing friendships she maintained with several women have not been explored as important elements in her emotional life.[9]

Perhaps it is time to try another approach. At the risk of resorting to identity labelling with all its pitfalls, accounts of women's lives that deal directly with their relationships with other women tend to be written by lesbians. Lesbian historians such as Lillian Faderman and Martha Vicinus have explored women's passionate friendships and the homosocial world in which many women lived and worked in late nineteenth-century England and the United States. There is no comparable account of Australian women. Then there are the books about women who sustained very well-known friendships or who lived in openly sexual relationships: Suzanne Raitt's account of the complex relationship between Vita Sackville-West and Virginia Woolf, for instance, and Diane Souhami's biographies of the painter, Gluck, and that infamous pair, Gertrude Stein and Alice B. Toklas. But the problem of writing about women who distanced themselves from any connection with what was considered abnormal sexuality remains a touchy one.

A framed photograph stands on the desk beside my computer. It is an enlarged passport photo from another era, when the convention was for head and shoulders to rise as if out of a cloud, denying the existence of a body below. This is the photo taken when Mary Fullerton sailed to England to rejoin Mabel Singleton and her young son in 1922. In the late afternoon sun the blue screen of my computer has become a palimpsest, the hieroglyphics across it almost erased by my reflected face. My head and shoulders mimic the photographic convention of the portrait, disappearing into shadow beneath the neck of my T-shirt. The image vanishes as the sun moves behind a cloud, leaving only the words themselves.

The poems Mary Fullerton wrote to Mabel Singleton conveyed to me that the face in the 1922 photograph and the one reflected in the computer screen share a significant connection. The bodies erased from just above the breasts are symbolic of the position we both occupy in the world, although we are separated by almost a century. Women who desire and respond to the touch of other women are hardly represented in our culture even now, except in negative stereotypes that Mary did not seem to recognise as true to her experience any more than I do.

I call myself a lesbian; Mary Fullerton did not. Nor did she refer to herself – in the language of the early twentieth century – as an invert or even the more appealing term Sapphist. The love that she expresses to Mabel Singleton in the poems that were written for her eyes only is for a friend, even if that term is often embellished, as in the poem, 'In Solitude', in which she is described as 'beloved, immediate friend/ The chosen of my heart'.

American feminist historians writing in the 1970s, such as Carroll Smith-Rosenberg and Lillian Faderman, suggested that such women lived in blissful ignorance of the sexual (and deviant) dimension of their love until the category of the "homosexual" was created in and through the new "science" of sexology that flourished in the late nineteenth century.[10] But isn't this model too simplistic, even a bit condescending to those women, many of whom formed life-long partnerships but did not call themselves lesbian even after the category's entry into common parlance?

Smith-Rosenberg and Faderman also pointed out that passionate declarations of love were common among married women writing to female friends, even to sisters or cousins. In other words, language that would today be considered sexual was part of the discourse of affection of the time. This research has been invaluable in opening up a space for women's 'romantic friendships' to be considered outside the dominant medical and psychological models of "abnormal" sexuality. But it has also created another escape for conventional biographers to avoid dealing with unorthodox sexuality: it can be explained away as being just the language women used.

Is it possible, even today, to draw a clear and unambiguous line between female friendships and lesbian relationships? Graham Little, author of a book on friendship, described it as a relationship that 'doesn't quite become sexual',[11] but how do we define 'sexual', and would that definition apply across the borders of history, culture and gender? As a concept, sexuality is incapable of ready containment. As Eve Kosofsky Sedgewick says: 'To some people, the nimbus of "the sexual" seems scarcely to extend beyond the boundaries of discrete genital acts; to others, it enfolds them loosely or floats virtually free of them'.[12]

A poem I found among the loose pages of Mary Fullerton's papers made me question the ethics of using this private material, compelling and fascinating though it is. Unlike Miles Franklin, who protested she wanted to be left alone after her death but who made arrangements for a plethora of personal documents to be left to the Mitchell for posterity, Mary's personal papers arrived there without her prior consent. Called 'Biography' and handwritten in pencil when Mary was seventy-two, this poem was annotated 'After reading some recent biographies. M.E.F. Aug 13, '40'.

> Let us be glad we are not great,
> But merely hedge folk, you and I.
> So no inquisitor shall come
> To filch our privacy.
>
> Slanting our nature, bending us
> This way and that to suit his wit.
> Till we with our own effigy
> Would as a stranger sit.
>
> Or worse; the fear of us removed,
> – Our mouths incompetent in clay –
> Our psyche proved so mean that God
> Would toss the thing away.

I had to consider what my role could be in this exploration. Inquisitor? Voyeur? Of course I am both to some extent. But perhaps I could offer Mary Fullerton some kind of deal, an exchange. When I read the manuscript of her 'Memoirs' in the Mitchell Library I was struck by her statement that 'ideas, ripe or raw, are germinal. They somehow get into the breathing atmosphere of the world, and scatter themselves here and there in strangely unassociated places'.[13] I want to try to understand what ideas were in the air and how they might have been breathed in when Mary Fullerton and Mabel Singleton and Miles Franklin were alive. Daphne Marlatt wrote in 1990: 'History is not the dead and gone, it lives on in us in the way it shapes our thought and especially our thought about what is possible'.[14] We are shaped by our personal histories and the historical narratives that are available to us. 'What is possible' may simply limit us to traditional paths. But if we turn to history, to the stories that happen between the lines of the major narratives – stories like Mary's and Mabel's – new possibilities open up.

In return, perhaps I can offer Mary Fullerton a way of telling at least a version of her story that was not possible in her lifetime. She once said in a letter to Miles that writing a life 'can't be done, it daren't be done'.[15] I agree that any life story is partial and slanted, even fictional, but it's the notion of 'daren't' that is revealing. After Mary's death, at the urging of Miles Franklin, Mabel Singleton tried to tell their story but could not. In a letter to Miles she said, 'I want to tell you all the story of our friendship before I try to write what can be told to the world at large'; later she wrote, 'It would be called "Stranger than Fiction"!!' Finally, in 1953, Mabel gave up the attempt, saying, 'What a story if it could be told'.[16]

Positive, though still marginal constructions of friendship and desire have emerged as a result of feminist theory of the last three decades. With the assistance of some of these, I shall 'dare' to tease out one version of the story of Mary Fullerton's life and her friendship with Mabel Singleton. Mary's friendship with Miles Franklin provides a counterpoint to this, while the two women's different negotiations of their commitment to chastity illuminates it in another way. The relationship between Mary and Mabel is also intertwined with their friendship with Miles and the network of women that surrounded them.

MARY

M-ary. She's complex and simple and witty and wise
A-s foolish as God ere created
R-ather stern of the mouth, and kind as to eyes,
Y-ea to paradox queerly related,
E-ver prim and consistent yet changeful as well
F-ull of faults with virtue confusedly mated,
U-rgent – and idle sometimes for a spell
L-oving and cynical; beloved too and hated,
L-oyal unto friend, and cold unto foe
E-ager to live, yet of pleasure soon sated,
R-ash, and yet cautious impulsive and slow
T-o dogma derisive, to truth dedicated
O-ptimist, pessimist – life seems to her so –
N-ot of much performing, but ne'er subjugated.

[Acrostic, no date]

In her unpublished 'memoirs', the typescript of which I spent several hours reading in the Mitchell Library, Mary Fullerton gently mocked the prevailing notion that autobiographies should only be written by important public figures or by those who had led adventurous lives: 'I have never climbed a mountain or sailed in a wind-jammer. There have been no startling events in my life. Only my mind has climbed, and striven with strong waves. Outward happenings have been few. Not worth chronicalling [sic] in a world where hair-raising adventures and experiences are so frequent that they cease to raise the hair'.[1] Mary's jibe, written when she was in her seventies, was directed at the undervaluing of women's lives and achievements because they tended to be less spectacular than men's.

The only part of her life Mary did write about (that is, in work intended for publication) was her childhood in Victoria's isolated and wildly beautiful North Gippsland region in the 1870s. Her best-known book is *Bark House Days*, a series of short autobiographical sketches written in her early fifties when she was in poor health herself and looking after her ill mother in Melbourne. The book stands as a punctuation mark in Mary Fullerton's life, its deliberately nostalgic, poetic style an elegiac farewell to childhood. It is a tribute to the place of bark hut and bush, and to the time she was to consider 'the most important period' of her life: 'the days that formed me, made me, for good or ill, the woman I am'.[2] 1921, the year *Bark House Days* was published, was also the year Mabel Singleton departed for England and the year Eliza Fullerton died. In January 1922, Mary started on a new journey when she left Australia to rejoin Mabel.

The 'Memoirs' Mary wrote in England in the late 1930s were intended to be the first part of a 'triptych' in which she would map her life according to its three distinct geographical locations – Gippsland, Melbourne and England. Only the Gippsland part was written. This time she did not recreate the child's perspective as she had in *Bark House Days*, but recorded her family history, in particular the contribution of pioneering women like her mother; she also reflected philosophically on the impact of those days on her own life. In this work, she traces her feminism, nationalism and socialist politics all back to her upbringing in that tight-knit settler community of Scots-Irish Presbyterians.

Later, I was to find almost identical stories of her early childhood in the first part of her anonymously-published semi-autobiographical novel, *Clare*, published in England in 1923. According to her usual pattern, she did write about her childhood, after which the novel follows a fictional plot. Recalling Mary Fullerton's comment to Miles Franklin that writing a life 'can't be done, it *daren't* be done', I am tempted to surmise that she restricted her autobiographical writing to her childhood because she found it impossible to write publicly about her significant relationship with Mabel Singleton. She had a horror of 'indiscreet memoirs', but she also lacked a language in which to write of her love for her friend and their long life together.[3]

Robert Fullerton and Eliza Leathers arrived at Port Melbourne in 1853 within two days of each other. They were not to meet until ten years later on the Ballarat gold fields, where they married soon after. Eliza, Mary's English mother, was fourteen when she and her parents reached Australia after a gruelling six month sea journey. At first the family lived in a tent city on the banks of the Yarra River. Many immigrants died in that "Canvas Town", where sandy blight, colonial fever (as typhoid was known then) and dysentery were rife. For the young middle-class girl from Suffolk, it must have been a testing introduction to the country in which she was to spend the rest of her life. Mary was to admire deeply her mother's tenacious spirit and the way she later held her own large family together through years of poverty and privation: her mother, she said, was 'the kind of gentlewoman who pulled up her socks and went at it. So much more remarkable, one with refined traditions than just a rough type. That of course is one of the telling facts about our Aus[tralian] pioneering women, so many of them doing so valiantly who had come from a different kind of life'.[4]

Mary's Celtic heritage, which she regarded as the source of her poetic imagination, came from her father's side of the family. So did the strict Presbyterian upbringing received by the six daughters and one son of Robert and Eliza Fullerton, although Mary was later to turn her back on orthodox religion, preferring her own idiosyncratic mix of mysticism and scepticism: 'I hate the cramping of creed . . . I prefer a certain vagueness'.[5] Her father's family were lowland Scots who had migrated several generations earlier to Belfast. Robert left Ireland for Australia as a young man, accompanied by his sister Lizzie, to try his fortune on the gold fields in the "New World". Lizzie was eventually to marry and settle next to the Fullertons at Glenmaggie and her sons were the boy cousins with whom Mary and her closest sister, Lydia (Claribel of *Bark House Days*), enjoyed a rough and tumble childhood. They explored the deep gullies, climbed trees, dropped worms into the waterhole to entice out eels, and played improvised cricket matches 'defending an old kerosene-tin from the onslaught of a rag ball'.[6]

The small settlement of Glenmaggie where Mary Fullerton spent the first twenty-five years of her life was situated on a 'selvage of rich farm land' along a river valley, 'skirting the hills that hugged the valley in a kind of jostling embrace, as though trying to push it back to the water's edge'.[7] The second surviving child of four, she was born there on 14 April 1868.[8] She and her siblings – 'the whole, wild, shy, little seven of us'[9] – grew up in the rough but capacious bark house her father, with the help of Uncle William, had built for his growing family on his small holding on the banks of Glenmaggie creek.

Nearly three decades before, immigrants from the Scottish Highlands had forged their way across the Australian Alps south from the Monaro region of New South Wales. Attracted by the diversity of the land with its rugged mountains, stands of tall timber and abundant lakes and rivers, Angus MacMillan called the region 'Caledonia Australis', but the Polish explorer, Paul Strzelecki, who led an expedition in 1840, succeeded in having it officially named Gipps Land after the Victorian governor, Sir George Gipps. By the mid 1840s there were forty stations in the region, mostly taken up by Scottish squatters.

Robert Fullerton took up his selection there in 1865 after a gold-mining venture, in which he was a partner, collapsed. In doing this, he joined the many immigrants with limited means who took up selections in rural Victoria after the passing of the Selection Acts – 'the product of an attempt to create an Australian independent yeomanry'.[10] The scheme was designed to settle the south-east part of a new continent – regarded then as *terra nullius* – in order to make it productive in European terms. The region that became known as Gippsland had, in fact, held 2–3,000 members of five Kurnai tribes, hunter-gatherers whose culture had remained unchanged for 6,500 years. By 1856, sixteen years after white settlers had crossed the Dividing Range, there were only 100 Aboriginal people left in the whole of Gippsland, the rest fallen victim to massacres, venereal disease and pulmonary infections that had raged through the black community. None of this is recorded in Mary Fullerton's writing, for she took on the prevailing ideas of Social Darwinism that considered the indigenous people of the continent to be a primitive and

21

dying race. In *Bark House Days*, she romanticises the 'strange hieroglyphs' on the trunk of an old box tree as being 'the illiterate, prehistoric signatures of roving aborigines, cut in by their tomahawks'.[11]

In 1872, when Mary was four years old, school attendance was made compulsory in Victoria for children between the ages of seven and thirteen. Glenmaggie did not get its first schoolhouse until Mary was seven and a half, and small though it was, it sported the first galvanised iron roof to be seen in the district. She remembers coming over the hilltop with her sisters and cousins on the day it opened, their eyes 'positively dazzled by the beauty and brightness of the roof flashing in the sun'.[12] There were 104 children under that roof on the first day, seated in rows in front of just one teacher, a young fair-haired woman whose violet eyes, Mary said, 'made a secret poet of me'.[13] Fortunately perhaps for the teacher, these children of the pioneer settlers often played truant or were kept at home by their parents when there was 'a push of work on the farm' such as potato-picking, which was regarded as child's work.[14]

Mary's school days came to an abrupt end when she was thirteen, after the School Inspector presented her with a form saying that she was 'according to the act sufficiently educated'.[15] She did not let this deter her passion for knowledge, but set about organising for herself a den in the wash house at the farm. Padlocking herself in for hours at a time, she devoured any books she could lay her hands on: the essays of Macauley, Hazlitt, and Lamb from an uncle's library, the macabre tales of Edgar Allan Poe from a neighbour's shelves. At one stage she was given the poems of Shelley as a present. In *Bark House Days* she claims to have read Milton's 'Paradise Lost' three times by the time she was eleven: 'rather a queer feat for a child I since find'.[16] She read Australian poets, Adam Lindsay Gordon and Henry Lawson, describing the latter in 'Memoirs' as 'a Homer, a Chaucer in moleskins';[17] she also became a devotee of the newly-established *Bulletin* – an influential nationalist magazine in which she later published – when copies were sent to the family by one of her uncles. In the 1870s she developed what was to be a life-long interest in what she called the psychology of crime through reading 'The Crimes and Trials of Victoria' in one of the Melbourne weeklies.

This eclectic and somewhat random self-education encouraged in Mary Fullerton a life-long habit of reading in a wide range of fields, in fact her knowledge was probably broader than that of many more privileged children who received a more structured schooling. Yet she remained sensitive, particularly among other writers, about her lack of formal education; it was probably one of the reasons she published her later poetry under the pseudonym 'E'. Their shared lack of a university education was to become a strong bond in her friendship with Miles Franklin; in their letters they often made jibes about the intellectual pretensions of academically-trained fellow writers like Marjorie Barnard and Flora Eldershaw.

Another bond between the two that helped mitigate their educational shortcomings was a shared sense of humour, which was often barbed as well as witty. 'If we could only talk', Mary wrote to her friend on one occasion, 'how much we could say. I think one thing that knits us is our sense of humour, it seems to be about identical. We are like the jackass in the Bush book too in that we can in the evening laugh over the fire that singed our tail in the morning'.[18] Her love of puns is evident throughout her correspondence with Miles; after a drubbing from a critic, she wrote: 'So old girl to be published is not all joy – when one is *peccable* and *peckable*'.[19]

Mary's closest sister was born just over a year after her own birth and so, at nighttime, the older child became her 'father's baby' while her mother attended to the new infant. But, she recalled in the fictional guise of the narrator of *Clare*, 'some deep thing in me, notwithstanding, has always made my mother more to me than he, the midnight pacer of the floor on my behalf, has ever been'. Her affection for her father was 'not of demonstrative quality' whereas with her mother she could not help demonstrating her affection. She concludes that 'the difference was significant of the strong predilection for my own sex that later came out in me so definitely'.[20]

It was watching her mother's situation that awakened Mary's feminism at an early age too. 'The first sprouting of this some-how-sown seed' occurred during a General Election when the illiterate farm-hands went off to vote while her own intelligent and educated mother was ineligible: 'I felt that somehow, prima-rily my mother was slighted and at large, Woman'. From that time Mary Fullerton became 'a little Mary Wollstonecraft'.[21] A photo-graph of Eliza Fullerton in the La Trobe collection features the same intense, light-coloured eyes and thin, determined mouth that her daughter inherited. Many years later Mary was to write, cryptically: 'My inner nature is a kind of contrast to my outward appearance – unless you study my grim mouth. (A man who once wanted to hate me said that my mouth would hang a man but my eyes would reprieve him'.)[22]

Poetry was an inspiration to the shy and introspective child who had not begun to talk until she was four years old. She began to 'string rhymes' at an early age and her efforts went into the 'poetry box' under the big bed she shared with 'Claribel' in their skillion bedroom at one end of the bark house.[23] Only Mary and her sister had access to this box. In 1880, at twelve years old, she had her first poem published when 'Under the Wattles' appeared in *Trafalgar Journal*, a Gippsland newspaper. She then bombarded 'more important publications' like the Mel-bourne newspapers and got many rejections.

At seventeen, Mary first made the hundred mile journey to the city of Melbourne with her uncle. 'I think that Melbourne disappointed me . . . I was too Romantic', recalled the vora-cious reader, who had expected something like 'Kubla Khan or Byron's Venice'.[24] Despite the guilt induced by 'the Puritan tra-dition' of her upbringing where even card-playing was frowned upon, she was transported by her first visit to the theatre to see a production of the nineteenth-century English melodrama, *Jim the Penman*.

The distance between bush and city diminished when the railway line was extended to the nearby town of Heyfield in 1887, after which Mary and members of her family made fre-quent trips to Melbourne. By her early twenties, she was having some success getting articles and poems published in various newspapers. 'Hungry for mental contacts' and anxious to continue her writing and perhaps pursue a career as a journalist, Mary made the move to Melbourne in about 1893: 'half way through my twenties; high time for a move, if ever to be made'.[25] Two of her sisters, Annie, the eldest, and her childhood playmate Lydia ('Claribel'), had by this time married and left home. Soon after their third daughter's departure, Robert and Eliza Fullerton and the three youngest daughters joined her in Melbourne, leaving the farm in the hands of their only son, Will. For several years they all lived in the suburb of Prahran, where Mary's father died in 1901. Six years later, the remaining all-female household bought Arden, a modest timber house in Hawthorn.

When Mary moved to Hawthorn with her mother and sisters, Emily, Sophia and Isabel (known as Em or Pem, Soph and Bell), she was thirty-nine years old. She had, through diligence and sheer dedication, largely succeeded in the goals she had set herself when she left Gippsland. Her papers in Mitchell Library record prizes won for her poems and stories; she attended literary meetings and, on occasions, overcame her shyness to deliver lectures about literature and feminism. Her papers in La Trobe Library include the text of a lecture she gave to the South Melbourne Women's Progressive League in 1903. Entitled 'Character in Women', she quotes from Byron, Pope, Chesterfield and Shakespeare to support her contention, familiar to feminists of today's generation, that all women are treated alike while men are individually differentiated.

She was also preparing her first book of sonnets and lyrics, *Moods and Melodies*. It was printed in 1908 at her own expense, customary at the time for poetry. Her profession is listed on the electoral roll as 'journalist' at a time when women journalists were paid only about half the amount received by their male counterparts. Her articles, short stories and poems printed in newspapers such as the *Weekly Times* and *The Leader* brought in a meagre living.

Mary's early-awakened political consciousness flourished

in Melbourne where she was active on several fronts in the area of social reform, but most particularly in women's rights. Her first association with prominent political activist and feminist, Vida Goldstein, came about when she contributed poems and articles to Goldstein's suffragist newspaper, *Woman's Sphere*, which ran from 1900 to 1905. Then, when Vida formed the Women's Federal Political Association in 1903 (it dropped the 'Federal' a year later), Mary began her long connection with the organisation. Through that work she met the woman who became her life-long partner.

In 'Memoirs', Mary Fullerton included a chapter entitled 'On Not Falling in Love', in which she claimed to have always enjoyed the company of men but that she had 'never wanted more than intellectual touch with the opposite sex': 'At the first indication of sentiment or "philandering" I've always been off like a shot'.[26] There is absolutely no indication that she formed any attachments with men during during her twenties and thirties, the years she lived and worked in Melbourne .

I did discover, though, in the collection of Mary's papers held in La Trobe Library, a series of exercise books containing handwritten poems and short stories (or 'sketches') she composed in the early 1900s when she was becoming involved in the Women's Political Association. They are curious pieces, hard to comprehend today, but it is possible to discern a recurring theme: the search for the woman who is the poet's destiny, her complement and soul-mate. The word "soul" is not often used now, but traces of its importance as a concept surface when we try to articulate profound emotions. When Mary Fullerton was writing, it was widely believed that the body was simply a temporary covering for the soul – the essence of a person that would live on after death. Soul was considered to be of a higher order than sense, spirit more significant than flesh.

Mary echoes this hierarchy in a series of poems she wrote on a trip to Glenmaggie in April 1904. Although she does not specifically gender the subject of many of these poems, their context among the stories in the exercise books leaves me in no doubt that the beloved the poet refers to is a woman. Their personal nature also makes it very unlikely that Mary herself was adopting a male voice. 'Was It Meant?', dated 25th April, draws more from a kind of cosmic mysticism than Christian doctrine:

> Was it meant we should meet?
> When you latent in cloud
> With fire from the sun
> Were spirit-endowed.
>
> Was it meant we should meet?
> When the atoms in space
> Clothed over your spirit
> A form and a face.
>
> Was it meant we should meet?
> When the dawn of your soul
> Thrilled to love, was my heart
> Its predestined goal? . . . [27]

In this poem, it seems that the spirit is made flesh before the soul, while the soul only 'dawns' when it is awakened by the thrill of love. The poet later answers her question, 'Was it meant?', with a suggestion that the senses are also an integral part of love. The hierarchy of soul and sense is maintained, but with the difference that love's meaning is confirmed through the senses. The poem continues:

> Yes twas meant we should meet
> For my hot heart in bliss
> Drew you in and the meaning
> Was clear in a kiss.

A prose sketch, called 'The Justification', that Mary wrote at the end of 1903, just a few months earlier than 'Was It Meant?', casts some light on this complicated construction of soul and sense, of friendship and desire. The sketch focuses on the waning of love between Laura, a lawyer, and her friend Esma: 'Laura was one of those women who love individuals of their own sex with all the intensity with which most women love individuals of the opposite sex. Hers was a deep intense nature, some said cold, but a few knew that the surface seeming was but the crust over the lava, beneath which lay rosy impetuous fires of everlasting love and tenderness –. Everlasting! Were they? That was Laura's puzzle on this mellow evening that seemed made for pensiveness and reflection'.[28]

In this piece, Laura goes through possible reasons for her emotional defection as if she is putting herself on trial, admitting: 'There was no one who sat as a new Deity on the altar, the fire had simply died down, leaving the Beloved strange and grieved, puzzled and dumbly reproachful'. She eventually comes to the conclusion that what she had felt was not a love of the soul: 'Esma's is that surface beauty over a shallow soul and vacant mind that draws all to whom Beauty appeals a little while – but for a little while only'. In the end, both are absolved: Laura of inconstancy, Esma because her 'shallow soul' is due to an inheritance beyond her control. Mary Fullerton believed that the potential of individual souls was innately variable. What is at stake is deeper than might be suggested by a reading that sees simply an account of a fleeting and purely physical attraction.

Immediately after 'The Justification', several pages are torn out of the exercise book, then the end of a poem appears at the beginning of the next page:

> And she left me alone, all alone, ah alone,
>   No lover or friend
> No name and no place, no passion, or pride
>   Awaiting the end.

Under it is written, 'M.E.F. Sunday 29.11.03'.

Although Mary Fullerton composed the series of poems that included 'Was It meant? before she met Mabel Singleton, the fantasy lover she writes of foreshadows uncannily some of the practical details of their situation, such as the fact that Mary was older than her lover by nearly a decade and that Mabel was born in a city on the other side of the world. On 10 April 1904 she wrote two poems – 'Mate!' and 'The Complement'. The first speaks of 'you' for whom 'life sang the day that you were born' while

> I far away an older child
>   In sleep
> Felt you and in my dreaming smiled
>   A-deep
>   . . .

> I knew you and I was content
> > To wait
> Till I should find you as was meant
> > By Fate

In the second poem written that day, the narrator writes 'I grew among the hidden hills' while 'You grew among the city's sounds' where you 'Dreamed of the grass that grew afar/ Where Nature's dim recesses are'. They meet:

> We passed each other in the street
> Looked back, and lingered, turned to meet
>
> Hands touched, and in a pulse we knew
> The heart's deep likeness of we two
>
> Grown out of divers ways akin
> At once the complement and twin
>
> . . .
>
> Life sought to make us alien souls
> Of diverse passions, foreign goals
>
> Environed us in ways apart
> But Nature gave to us one heart
>
> Such if they meet can recognize
> Through every difference and disguise
>
> That fortunes two, are Nature's one
> And thus Life's tangles are undone.[29]

Is this a prophetic fantasy, or just a strange coincidence? The poet may be writing about a different younger woman, one who grew up in Melbourne and with whom she had fallen in love. A sonnet called 'Recognition', written after Mary met Mabel, suggests she may not have been the first woman to attract her:

> The years were kind that hid you till I grew
> Wiser to know you when to parallel
> Our roads came quietly, and my soul could tell
> That all the minor loves it ever knew
> Were meant to lead me grandly up to you,
> To put my hand in yours as has befell.
> And oh the hour was come to *know* as well –
> The hour that flashed Life's meaning, and the clue . . .

A poem I found among Mary Fullerton's papers in the Mitchell Library clearly indicates that she eventually found the soul-mate she'd searched for. It is typed on the same page as one called 'Dearness', which appeared in the collection published in 1921, dedicated 'To My Friend Mabel Singleton'. 'Hearthome', written for Mabel's eyes only, was not published:

> Heartward come to my arms,
> Now I have found you;
> Long, long ago ere I saw you
> My love was around you.
>
> Soul-led I have pursued,
> Now I behold you;
> Won from the dream and the vision –
> Thus I enfold you.
>
> Heart-close rest in my arms,
> – Destinies bind you;
> Else o'er the earth and the oceans
> How did I find you?

MABEL AND MILES

> Did I tell you your 30/– has gone towards the typing of
> Mary's Life Story. I am putting the balance . . .
>
> *[PS to a letter from Mabel Singleton to*
> *Miles Franklin, ca 1939]*

I f I searched in vain for any mention of Mabel Singleton in
Mary Fullerton's 'Life Story', her 'Memoirs', I did find a reference in its pages that held familiar resonances. Mary recalls:

> I was once, many years ago, reading some poetry to a
> small child less than five years of age. "I can make poetry",
> said he suddenly. "Yes" – and I waited. He thought for a
> minute and then I had this –
>
> > The waves dash on the shore,
> > The waves dash more and more,
> > Until the night comes stealing by.
>
> "That's poetry", he said. I agreed, and asked what name he
> would give the poem. At once came "Harry sees it". "That",
> he explained, "is because I do see it." The very essence of
> the matter.
>
> The remarkable thing about this is that from that time
> (it was twenty-five years ago) I have never known during
> an intimate acquaintance with the 'infant poet' any fur-
> ther inspiration show itself. Indeed, he has grown up
> without the least liking for poetry. He trailed his little cloud
> of glory, and was done with it.[1]

Turning to the unpublished poems I had copied from the Mitchell collection (poems that were written several decades before
'Memoirs'), I found what I was looking for:

> The waves dashed to and fro
> Upon the rocky shore;
> The waves dashed more and more,
> Until the night came passing by.

This very similar piece was called 'Denis Sees It'.

Mabel Singleton's son, Denis, was filling my sherry glass when he announced, 'I must show you a photograph of Mater because she was a very beautiful woman. I'll go and get it'. I could hardly believe my luck. Not only had I found the 81-year-old Denis alive and well on my visit to London in 1992 when the Guide to the Mary Fullerton Papers in the Mitchell Library had pronounced him dead in the 1960s, I was about to see a photo of the woman whose beauty Mary praised in so many poems. I had, it is true, found a snapshot of mother and son on an English beach (near Folkestone, according to Denis) in the Miles Franklin Papers, taken in 1933. But the rather stern-looking matron seated stiffly on a rug in coat and broad-brimmed hat bore little resemblance to the beloved of the poems, save perhaps for the well-defined cheekbones and aquiline nose.

Those features of classical beauty were clearly in evidence in the studio portrait Denis proudly handed me, taken more than thirty years earlier than the beach snapshot. As I met the young Mabel Jupp's dark eyes gazing steadily from the photograph's oval frame, I recalled the words of a sonnet Mary Fullerton wrote at Glenmaggie on 1 November 1910, soon after their meeting:

> I cannot think it was an English sun
> That put those glowing colours in your veins.
> Not the calm influences of hedgey lanes,
> Made the soft shine to your smooth cheek run;
> I cannot think that where that flower is spun
> We call the primrose, born of dews and rains
> Those rich dark eyes' audacity was won
> Whose languors and whose mysteries seem Spain's . . .

Acutely aware of the sensitive nature of my mission to find out more about Mary Fullerton and Mabel Singleton's relationaship, I did not read this love poem aloud to the elderly couple who were so eager to share their memories. Had those passionate words been written by a male suitor, I would not have skirted carefully around their implication.

Mabel's portrait bore on the back of it the address, 'Lichfield Rd, Walsall'. She was born there, in the Black Country of the industrial West Midlands in England, on 9 September 1877. ('I grew among the hidden hills . . . You grew among the city's sounds', wrote Mary in 1902). Little is known of Elizabeth Mabel Ethel Jupp's life in Walsall or of her family background. The occupation of her father, Richard Jupp, is listed as tailor on her birth certificate. Her mother, Elizabeth, died at the age of 45 when Mabel was 21, information I gleaned from a letter Mabel wrote to Miles Franklin after the death of Miles's mother in 1938.[2] Mr Jupp remarried, but Mabel was to say she had little in common with his second wife.

Mabel Jupp remained single until a relatively late age for the early 1900s. On 18 October 1904, just after her 27th birthday, she married Australian resident, Robert Singleton, at the Registry Office in Kensington, London. The bridegroom was a 63-year-old widower who had fathered six children, several of whom were older than his new wife. I wondered why Mabel had married a man nearly four decades her senior. And with such little ceremony. Denis has no idea.

Details about Robert Singleton are sketchy, but his father had been a Clerk in Holy Orders, said to have arrived in Australia in 1849 when the young Robert would have been eight years old. Retired Chief Accountant with the Victorian Railways at the time of his marriage to Mabel Jupp, Robert Singleton was rumoured to have amassed his considerable fortune from the discovery of a gold reef in the 1860s.[3] It is possible Mabel might simply have loved this man, but it is also possible his wealth helped persuade her to marry him; perhaps the idea of living in a country on the other side of the world was attractive to her too.

Some time in 1905 the young Englishwoman travelled to Australia with her husband to live in his mansion, Haverbrack, in the Melbourne suburb of Malvern. Built in 1854, Haverbrack had been owned by Robert Singleton for many years and it had been his home during his first marriage to Sabina Embling. The tiny snapshot Denis Singleton showed me was of a large, single-storey house with a sweeping circular drive. It had apparently been surrounded by acres of gardens, croquet lawns and an orchard, part of which had been sold before Mabel took up residence there.

If the beautiful young Mabel Singleton was intended to play the part of gracious hostess to her elderly husband's guests at Haverbrack, she does not seem to have found it a role that suited her. Political activism was much more her style and this became a strong element of her life in Melbourne. We might conjecture she had been involved in the suffragist movement in England before her marriage. The first mention of Mabel Singleton's name I have found in connection with the Women's Political Association occurs in a handwritten list of names at the back of Vida Goldstein's 1908 diary, but it was to be another two years after that before her path would cross that of Mary Fullerton.[4] Whatever unknown conditions were set when Mabel Jupp entered into marriage with the man who was thirty-six years her senior, Denis is certain about one. Robert Singleton insisted he wanted no more children.

Denis Singleton remembers Miles Franklin well from the time she shared their home at 181c High Street in the early 1930s, when he was twenty-one years old. 'But funnily enough', he told me, 'I have no recollection of her in Melbourne when I was a child although I must have met her many times'. I explained to him that, although their friendship was so important in their later lives, Mary Fullerton and Miles Franklin never knew each other in Australia but had met in London in the early 1920s. Denis and Eileen were most surprised, probably because being "Australian" writers was such a key connection between the two women. Part of the strength of that connection had been their rural upbringing and the 1890s nationalist fervour in Australia. Mary and Miles both took on the reverence for the Australian bush pioneers that was fostered in magazines like *The Bulletin* and reworked that through a feminist lens.

Stella Miles Franklin was the youngest of the three friends of this story, two years younger than Mabel Singleton and eleven years Mary Fullerton's junior. She was born in 1879 in the Monaro in New South Wales and spent the first ten years of her life on her parents' property at Talbingo in the Brindabella Ranges, on the edge of what is now the Australian Capital Territory. Educated at home and then at a bush school after her parents moved to a property in the Goulburn district, she, like Mary, left before high school as it was not considered necessary for girls to receive a secondary education.

Small and dynamic, with luxuriant long dark hair that she took great pride in, the young Stella Franklin had many talents. She was a gifted horsewoman and became well-known as a local show-rider. A neighbour recalled how she used to race the train into Goulburn on her horse, adding, 'She loved a joke'.[5] Stella also developed a striking contralto singing voice which was, however, irrevocably damaged through incorrect training, a tragedy she was to write about many years later in her novel, *Cockatoos*. Stella appears very different from the reticent Mary Fullerton but she did share with Mary the kind of shyness peculiar to country children, a legacy they were both later to feel keenly in the literary world where a veneer of sophistication was *de rigeur*.

Stella Franklin adopted her second name, Miles, as a pseudonym to protect knowledge of her gender when, at eighteen, she wrote her first and best-known novel, *My Brilliant Career*. In what was to be their most historic mistake, Angus & Robertson rejected the manuscript of *My Brilliant(?) Career* in 1899. It was eventually published, with the assistance of Henry Lawson and London literary agent, J.B. Pinker, by Blackwood of Edinburgh in 1901. The young author's desire 'to pose as a bald-headed seer of the sterner sex' was thwarted by Lawson when he announced in his preface to the first edition that the book was by 'a girl'.[6] This older Australian writer's assistance proved to be a mixed blessing; he revised and cut the manuscript without Miles Franklin's permission, while the publishers deleted the all-important ironical question mark from the title.

To Miles's consternation, the story of the rebellious Sybylla Melvyn, a fine horsewoman who falls in love with the eminently suitable Harry Beecham but refuses to marry him because she wants to become a writer, was assumed by critics and acquaintances of the family to be autobiographical. While there were significant elements of Miles herself in the character of Sybylla and the Melvyn family bore a close resemblance to the Franklins, *My Brilliant Career* was in no way a piece of documentary realism. A cry from the heart about the position of young Australian women in the late nineteenth century, it was also intended to parody the popular romance genre with its overwrought language and melodramatic situations. To make her point clearly, Miles used the structure of the romantic novel while abandoning its traditional resolution. Such fictional additions as Sybylla's father's heavy drinking were a particular source of dismay to the author's family.

Although the reception of *My Brilliant Career* led to Miles' decision that it should not be reprinted in her lifetime, the novel also received much critical praise for the outspokenness that set it apart from any previously written by Australian women. It inspired many personal letters by women who found resonances of their own situation in its pages. One letter of praise was from the influential Sydney feminist, Rose Scott, who wrote, rather pompously, to Miles in 1902 after reading *My Brilliant Career*: 'Your book is so life like, I cannot disassociate yourself from the heroine . . . Let me my dear fellow Australian, my dear fellow woman, serve you in any way I can'.[7] After the Franklin family moved to Penrith at the foot of the Blue Mountains outside Sydney in 1903, Rose Scott, over thirty years Miles's senior, took the young writer under her wing, introducing her to the world of women's rights activism. At Miss Scott's "salon" – the famous Friday night gatherings held in her Woollahra home – Miles met activists, politicians, artists, and writers as well as 'shy girls in high-necked frocks from the country or outer suburbs' not unlike herself.[8]

The relationship between the two women was the first of several long-standing friendships that Miles was to cultivate with older single women, friendships that significantly influenced her own life-long rejection of marriage. In an article on Rose Scott, written for Flora Eldershaw's *The Peaceful Army* in 1938, Miles outlined the qualities she admired in her friend and mentor, stressing the fact that Miss Scott's unmarried state was a choice and not because she was plain or unwomanly: 'Rose Scott had beauty and charm. She was the personification of all that was most desirable and commendable in femininity. This must be stressed, for in Rose Scott's earlier decades woman's place was still the home in the restrictive sense. A woman who *did not* choose to marry was the target of slurs that she *could not*. A woman who wanted to develop her mental powers above those of a hen or a doll was *unsexed* . . . Rose Scott's womanly attractions were such that the most blatant males could not accuse her of *couldn't* in the matrimonial sense. They could only moan that she *hadn't*, and what a loss it was to some man'.[9]

Miles Franklin was always sensitive to her own position as an unmarried woman and was terrified of being thought abnormal, hence the importance of role-models who remained spinsters while not in any way compromising their 'femininity'. Deeply influenced by the prevailing idea that the intellect was the prerogative of men and that clever women were 'unsexed', she protested against the notion and its repercussions for women all her life. In 1947 she informed Vida Goldstein's sister, Aileen, that 'men who approached me in my nubile decades always, when defeated, accused me of being sexless, of being not a woman but a mind'.[10]

In 1904, Miles Franklin was in Melbourne, gathering background for a book by doing a stint as a domestic servant. This was a time when Miles and Mary Fullerton might have met, but apparently did not. Mary was then a regular contributor to *Woman's Sphere*, Vida Goldstein's suffragist paper, and the April edition of the magazine ran an article on Miles Franklin, accompanied by a photograph of her dressed in her 'Mary Anne' maid's uniform. It described the unusual hands-on research the writer was undertaking as 'parlour-maid, housemaid, kitchen-maid, cook, nurse'.[11] Though the projected book never eventuated, this undercover research is an early example of Miles Franklin's life-long fascination with disguise, the most extraordinary manifestation of which was to take the form of her pseudonymous persona, Brent of Bin Bin. The article also relayed the history of the publication of *My Brilliant Career* for its Melbourne readers, commenting, 'There is a cry of fierce revolt in it, which is common enough among the dwellers in plain and mountain, but it has never before been given with such force as in this book'.

Miles certainly became well-acquainted with the Goldsteins

during her Melbourne sojourn. A letter from Vida, written in May 1904, thanks her for the offer of a short story for the paper and she also received letters from Vida's mother, Isabella, and her sister, Aileen.[12] The Goldstein women all endeavoured to convert Stella (as they always called her) to Christian Science and it seems she might have been a little tempted, at least at this stage of her life. Aileen Goldstein expressed her disappointment in a letter that Miles 'had decided to drop Science', but hoped that if she did go away to America (as Miles must have already been planning) she would meet some Scientists there.[13] Aileen and Vida continued intermittently to try to persuade Miles to embrace 'Science' and 'the life of the spirit' for the next forty years, but she remained a sceptic.

In April 1906, at 26 years old, Miles Franklin boarded the *SS Ventura* for the United States. Whatever her intentions when she left, she did not return to live permanently in Australia until 1933. Armed with introductions to American feminists from Vida Goldstein, who had toured America four years earlier, she reached Chicago at the end of 1906. There she met Alice Henry, a prominent Australian activist who had left Australia in 1905. Alice was another older woman who was to be influential in her life and Miles spent the next nine years working alongside her for the National Women's Trade Union League. Twenty-two years older than Miles, Alice Henry impressed the young woman with her strength of character: 'Miss Henry was tremendously true and staunch, . . . she never seemed to be afflicted by weaknesses or doubts'.[14] These were significant attributes to Miles who often suffered from severe depression during her years in Chicago, a problem that was to recur throughout her life.

Alice Henry seems to have led a totally work-orientated life. Her biographer reports it to be 'stunningly silent on the question of emotional or sexual involvements' and says there is no evidence to suggest that she was ever erotically involved with either man or woman.[15] The close friendships she maintained with her colleagues in the WTUL appear to have sustained her, her relationship with Stella (as Miles was always called by her American friends) becoming one of the most important.

It was through Alice Henry and Vida Goldstein that Miles Franklin was eventually to track down Mary Fullerton in London. In May 1922, Miles wrote to Alice that she had not met 'Miss Fullerton' yet: 'She was to have been at a dinner a week ago, but it fell through. I heard of her though. Vida was seeing her off at King's Cross for Letchworth and the train man came along and said of her typewriter, "What have you got there?" and when told she was made to pay 2/9 or some sum like that. She retorted, "I have a fountain pen, do you fine me for that also!"'.[16] Miles was later to tell Mary that she remembered Vida Goldstein 'laughing gaily' about her wit long before she met her.[17]

The network of women involved in politics in Melbourne in the early 1900s spread to the United States and the United Kingdom and its influence continued long after the vote was won. The political arena was to be important for women's networks later in the twentieth century too. Writing about the "second-wave" feminist movement in the 1970s and '80s, American feminist and academic Carolyn Heilbrun stressed the importance of feminist politics to women's friendships: 'The sign of female friendship is not whether friends are homosexual or heterosexual, lovers or not, but whether they share the wonderful energy of work in the public sphere. These, some of them hidden, are the friends whom biographers of women must seek out.[18] In this statement, Heilbrun was defending her position as a heterosexual woman at a time when "women-identified women" in lesbian relationships tended to claim their situation as the most superior form of female friendship. There was no such discourse in the women's rights movement at the beginning of the twentieth century, but many women involved shared intense friendships that were similar in many ways to those among later political lesbian feminists. I would suggest that shared political passions among feminists of any era make for a heady atmosphere of homosocial connection (Heilbrun's 'wonderful energy of work'), one in which the distinctions between the sexual and non-sexual become more than usually blurred.

SUFFRAGISTS AND PACIFISTS

The members of the Women's Political Association in Melbourne in the early 1900s were very much part of a female-centred environment. Formed along non-party lines by suffragist Vida Goldstein, the WPA specifically addressed the needs of women. The leading article in the first issue of its newspaper, *Woman Voter*, August 1909, declared that 'it is not to be supposed we are a body of gelatinous creatures', arguing that the Association's non-party stance was not a matter of indecisiveness but a conscious strategy. This was deemed necessary because issues relating to women and children were 'sacrificed to party interests in nine cases out of ten' by the established political parties.

The suffrage movement in Victoria, unlike that in Britain, never attracted the support of the wealthy. While Vida Goldstein herself was from an upper middle-class background and was educated at the Presbyterian Ladies' College in Melbourne, the lower middle class predominated among the rank and file of the WPA and the association always had a healthy support from country women. Unlike some of the more conservative women's organisations in Melbourne, the WPA's leanings were radical liberal. While still supporting the institution of marriage, for instance, they campaigned for equal pay to enable women to remain single and openly took on "delicate" issues such as the scourge of venereal disease and support for unmarried mothers. Many WPA members also became involved in the Victorian Socialist Party and some had associations with the Australian Church, formed by Charles Strong, which attracted many of Melbourne's progressive thinkers who were dissatisfied with traditional Christianity.

After much initial debate on the subject of whether men should be admitted as members of the WPA, it was decided they could join but not as policy-makers or office-bearers. Of the 707 foundation members in 1903, 652 were women and 55 men. There were nine men in a committee of twenty-two when the WPA first formed but the numbers quickly dwindled; after the first Annual

General Meeting, only three men remained. Of the female foundation members, almost half were unmarried. Nearly fifty of them were teachers; there were also business women, those working in trades and a few of the first women graduates from the University of Melbourne.[1]

Mary Fullerton and Mabel Singleton possibly knew each other by sight as members of the WPA before the spring of 1909, but it was in connection with Vida Goldstein's second attempt to become the first woman to enter Australian federal politics that they were brought into close contact. Vida had accepted the nomination of the WPA to stand for the Senate late in 1909; the *Woman Voter* recorded that 'Mrs R. Singleton has been appointed chairman, Miss M. E. Fullerton hon[ourable] sec[retary] of Miss Goldstein's Central Committee'.[2] Vida's campaign opened in Casterton in country Victoria in February 1910; Mary and Mabel addressed meetings in Melbourne while the candidate herself travelled around the Western District and Gippsland. They then campaigned intensively with her in Melbourne until the campaign wound up in Hawthorn on 12 April.

It seems likely that the 'place' referred to in Mary's 1911 poem, 'Anniversary', was the office they worked in, the campaign offices at Whitehall, Bank Place, Melbourne. Starting with the words, 'For two years I've loved you', it contains the lines:

> Two years since I met you
> In yonder dull place;
> Made beautiful then
> By your beautiful face.

In the poem Mary wrote for Mabel's birthday in 1912 – 'September 9th, 1912' – when the friends were holidaying at St Margaret's Bay near Dover, Mary recalls a 'Little Room' that was their meeting place:

> And so for these three years I thank the gods
>   That we have met, that we have met,
> For all their splendour, and the splendid pain,
>   The joy, the fret
> That mark our passage from that Little Room
>   *To this St Margaret's.*

41

I imagine Mary and Mabel must have spent many hours together at the campaign office in Bank Place, perhaps staying late to do the paper work involved in organising the more than twenty town and country local committees that took part in the election campaign. Was it on one of those occasions, on a long Melbourne Spring evening, that Mabel made the crucial move that was to acknowledge the intense feelings circulating between the two women? Mary recorded it in the last stanza of 'Anniversary':

> Dear heart I am grateful
> Your hand came to mine,
> Dear love are you glad that
> My clasp answered thine?

In an undated sonnet, Mary elaborates on a moment that may well have been the same one:

> Half a long evening, of your face I had
> Only its profile clear against the light,
> – A vital cameo on the breast of Night –
> Something then made my prescient being glad,
> Something compelled an ecstasy half sad;
> And I was filled with strange transcendent sight,
> Made wise to read the oracles aright:
> I was what some call sane, but most call mad.
>
> And then you turned your pregnant eyes on me,
> Touched my faint hand, and made of me your own,
> No words were relevant of Speech's treasury;
> The silence of your greatness called alone,
> My heart went to you with the stretching hand
> The eyes of both proclaimed "I understand".

As the intense friendship between the two women developed, Mary continued to live at Arden in Hawthorn with her mother and sisters, while Mabel resided a few miles away in Malvern with her elderly husband in the big house with the circular drive. They spent many hours in each other's company, however, even after the fervour of the political campaign, for the WPA provided a social as well as a political life for its members.

Over the years, it formed the WPA Operatic and Dramatic Society and the WPA choir. Regular 'At Home' evenings were held, where entertainment was provided by members: musical items, tales of travel and witty lectures. Mary Fullerton was a frequent lecturer; one of the topics she spoke on was 'Conventionality'. Sometimes the evening concluded with a dance. At one of these 'At Home' functions, Alice Henry, the Melbourne activist who was Miles Franklin's mentor and friend in Chicago, was voted one of 'the three most notable Australian women', along with Vida Goldstein and the novelist Catherine Helen Spence.[3]

Among the visitors from overseas who were entertained by the association was Miss Muriel Matters, a suffragette who had been imprisoned in Holloway Gaol and who made a lecture tour of Australia in 1910, accompanied by her friend, Miss Violet Tillard, who had also been in Holloway. Apparently, Muriel Matters scattered leaflets over London from a balloon at the opening of Parliament in 1909; on another occasion she chained herself to the grille of the Ladies Gallery in the House of Commons.[4] The WPA held a reception in the banquet room of Sargent's Café on 18 June for the two women and among those who delivered speeches 'welcoming the newcomers' were Vida Goldstein, Mary Fullerton and Mabel Singleton.[5]

The WPA had instituted its own Women's Parliament in 1904, with a Ministry elected by WPA members, holding weekly sessions between April and December. While providing a serious platform for members to develop their political skills, it also functioned on a social level. Sessions were sometimes combined with 'At Homes' and the debates were lively and often humorous affairs, where specific issues were introduced and discussed.

In August 1910, a Domestic Service Bill was introduced by the 'Prime Minister', Mabel Singleton, who emphasised that its principle was to raise domestic service to the level of a profession. The Bill had thirteen points, concentrating on training and conditions for the 'girls': all were to be over the age of seventeen, the Government was to provide accredited training courses, there was to be a fixed minimum wage, their living quarters were to meet certain specifications, hours of duty were set down, and Women Inspectors were to be appointed to visit homes where domestic help was employed.[6]

The fact that Mabel was later to run a domestic hiring agency in London for more than twenty years gives the subject of this debate a particular significance. That she still followed her feminist principles is obvious from this comment made by Mary in a letter to Miles Franklin in 1929: 'Mrs Singleton has been for several weeks without a secretary, going hard for about fourteen hours a day . . . It's hard to get suitable help at the office, chits are no use and older women usually want to run the bus[iness] themselves in a ghastly manner, inclined to treat the maids as dirt, the mistresses as goddesses. Against Mabel's principles hence difficulty in getting the right person'.[7]

The 1910 sittings of the Women's Parliament were held every Monday evening in Sargent's Café at 28 Elizabeth Street, in the heart of Melbourne, and the public were invited to attend. By 1917 they were held at the Guild Hall, perhaps a more formal venue, but it appears from reports such as this one in *Woman Voter* that the atmosphere of the sessions was still lively: 'Miss Kavanagh ([member for] West Sydney) asked the Prime Minister (Miss John), without notice, why she left West Sydney. (Roars of laughter). Prime Minister (Miss John): I left West Sydney so that my honourable friend might have the privilege of occupying the seat which she now fills so gracefully. (Roars renewed).'[8] An in-joke that only WPA members were privy to? The Prime Minister at this third Women's Parliament was Cecilia John; Mabel was now Minister for Peace and Mary Minister for Lands, while Vida Goldstein was elected Governor-General, Speaker and Chairman of Committee.

Given the "populate or perish" imperative of the early 1900s in Australia, the WPA addressed its major efforts towards improving conditions for women and children. The birth rate had been declining steadily since the 1890s with increasing urbanisation and more widespread use of contraception, particularly by educated middle-class women, and smaller families. From an average of seven or more children in 1891, women who began child-bearing in 1911 averaged only four. At the same time, calls for restricted immigration had been loudly voiced in the newspapers since the early 1890s when European immigration had begun to dwindle. *The Bulletin* was the most blatantly racist;

'Give the Yellow Man once firm foothold in the North and he will gradually overrun the continent' was typical of its warnings.[9] The WPA supported the White Australia Policy that was instituted in 1901 and considered Anglo-Saxon motherhood to be a social issue of critical importance. But racist though it was, the WPA's focus on motherhood was also feminist. It supported equal marriage and divorce laws, equal parental rights over children, and equal property rights after death.

The organisation was also critical of traditional representations of domesticity, and the title of Vida Goldstein's first newspaper, *Woman's Sphere*, was meant to indicate that 'sphere' included every facet of life, public as well as private. In line with this approach and contrary to the predominant thinking of the time, marriage and motherhood were not considered to be the ultimate goals for all women. On the contrary, women were encouraged to decide their particular destiny for themselves, whether it be as a mother or as a single woman. So equal pay and opportunities for employment were also important parts of the WPA's agenda.

Mary Fullerton's short story, 'A Dream', published in the *Woman Voter* in 1914, satirised the way women were relegated to the domestic sphere while it also extolled the value of traditional women's work, including motherhood.[10] In it, the narrator dreams, to her surprise and horror, that the WPA newspaper has introduced a women's column. This contains a knitting pattern for 'a dainty dinner jacket for your dog', advertisements for egg-whisks that can double as lawn-mowers, and a correspondent signing herself 'Anguish' is told why her pancakes are doughy. After realising she was dreaming, the narrator goes on to use the kinds of domestic metaphors such as 'Let us knit ourselves into the mesh with all humanity' and 'let the web of our life be of mingled yarn' that feminists of the 1970s and 1980s thought they had invented. During World War I, Mary was to publish an anti-war poem called 'Knitting' that uses domestic imagery to powerful effect:

> While the men fight and kill,
> With sword and pen;

They are knitting, knitting,
Women, the makers of men.

While men are tearing down
With the hell-rammed gun;
Woman is knitting, knitting,
As she has ever done.

Weaving while men destroy,
With sword and pen;
Women are knitting, knitting –
Knitting the shapes of men.

Silent with patient pain,
In the day and night;
Weaving new limbs and hearts
For the long sunlight.

Women, the makers of men,
The vessels of Life;
Oh! but the men are gods –
Makers of strife! [11]

Single women obviously thrived in the environment of the WPA, where many resisted the woman's role of wife and mother and contested society's stereotype of the spinster. Reporting on a lecture entitled 'Spinsters Indispensable', delivered to a meeting of the WPA in 1913, *Woman Voter* wrote that Miss K. Cornell 'kept her audience entertained by her quaint presentation of the masculine idea of the unmarried woman'.[12] Mary Fullerton also wrote on the subject of spinsters in a short story called 'The Superfluous Woman', in which a group of unmarried friends discuss the way spinsters like themselves are regarded as superfluous because they have not fulfilled the roles assigned to them by society. They point out that unmarried men do not suffer the same stigma; they also discuss the unfair laws that deny women equal pay and force many into loveless marriages simply to ensure their survival. One of the characters implores her friends not to 'get bitter', however, telling them 'that's the worst self-injury'.[13]

Close friendships such as that between Mary Fullerton and Mabel Singleton were often acknowledged in the pages of the

Woman Voter. When the two women went to England on a trip in 1912 (on 'a well-deserved holiday'), a farewell was held for them at the Austral Salon 'with flowers and refreshments'.[14] When they returned in 1913, an article simply headed 'Mrs Singleton and Miss Fullerton' welcomed 'two of our best workers' back into the fold.[15] And when Mary was forced to resign from the WPA in 1918 'owing to the ill-health of herself and her mother', the *Woman Voter* noted: 'Mrs Singleton and Miss Fullerton are at present taking a holiday at Point Lonsdale, where we may expect Miss Fullerton to find further poetic inspiration'.[16]

This holiday did, in fact, inspire a poem I found among those written for Mabel. Titled 'Evening' and dated February 1918, this poignant sonnet evokes a world-weariness that everyone must have felt after four years of war. It also expresses Mary's characteristic belief in the human spirit, perhaps strengthened by the fact that she was at the seaside in the company of her beloved friend:

> We face to where the west in reddening flare
> Burned our wild day upon the distant deep;
> And clouds drove to the sea like flocks of sheep
> Before the lightning's lash, till down the glare
> Stole gently grey-robed Eve, and everywhere
> Calmed Nature frighted by the tempest's leap
> Till mingled hill, and sea, and silenced air
> In one serene companionship of sleep.
>
> And then we turned away and went within,
> To talk of books and crowded themes of life;
> Our hearts with Nature's latest mood akin –
> – Dashed by the conquering knowledge of man's strife –
> Yet gently too that quiet sense felt fall,
> That human life is greater than it all.

Another prominent close friendship in the WPA, between Vida Goldstein and Cecilia John, flourished in the later years of the association's existence. In August 1913, a 'tall strong woman' with a 'magnificent contralto voice' performed at a social evening held by the WPA to honour Vida's hard-fought but unsuccessful election campaign for the seat of Kooyong.[17] Suddenly the pages of the *Woman Voter* were full of the name Cecilia John. She became Vida's secretary, then the WPA's business manager; under her management, the *Woman Voter* was enlarged and a direct cable link to the Women's Social and Political Union (WSPU) in London was established. Her rapid rise through the ranks of the WPA did not go unnoticed by other hard-working members, one of whom was heard to grumble, 'When Miss John wants a thing there does not seem anything to do but cave in'.[18]

When war broke out in 1914, Cecilia John was an instrumental force in the establishment of the Women's Peace Army. Formed by Vida Goldstein, it was to be closely connected with the WPA but devoted solely to peace propaganda. Vida's anti-militarist and anti-conscription stance had already created something of a split in the ranks of the WPA and some of the more conservative members, including the secretary and treasurer of the time, resigned in October. A resolution was passed in November that the WPA should alter the plank of its platform on International Peace to 'Opposition to Compulsory Military Training and Militarism', the vote being 22 to 8.[19] Among those supporting the controversial motion were Mary Fullerton and Mabel Singleton. They both spoke frequently at the anti-conscription rallies held at the Guild Hall and on the Yarra Bank during the following three years.

When the WPA bought fourteen acres of land at Mordialloc to establish a women's farm, Cecilia John was closely involved in the running of it. She provided expertise in raising poultry; the farm also produced white leghorns, reared cattle and grew produce that was sold at the WPA rooms. Women and girls were employed and trained on the farm, about six at a time, throughout the war. A reporter from the *Socialist* who visited the farm was quoted in *Woman Voter* as saying that 'the robust and ladylike girls . . . looked as intelligent and as healthful as it was possible to imagine'.[20]

The dynamic Cecilia finally resigned from the WPA and the Women's Peace Army in 1918 to devote more time to music. Later that year she set up the People's Conservatorium with Annie Macky, aiming to bring 'the world of art to the masses'.[21] A lasting image of Cecilia John as Chief Marshal in the spectacular Women's No-Conscription Demonstration and Procession of October

1916 remains in my mind from the description of the event in *Woman Voter*. A striking figure on horseback, she was dressed in white and carried a staff 'decorated in the purple, white and green colours of the WPA'.[22] Three young girls carrying banners led the procession in front of Cecilia John; she in turn was followed by the members of the Women's No-Conscription Committee, including Vida Goldstein, Mary Fullerton and Mabel Singleton. The procession from Guild Hall to the Yarra Bank included eight horse-drawn lorries with tableaux, lorries full of children, and many individuals on foot and in vehicles. At one point several dozen peace doves were released from the children's lorries.[23]

Accounts of Vida Goldstein's life report that 'a personal note is curiously absent' from her papers and correspondence.[24] It is as if the public persona of the neat, attractive woman, always immaculately and stylishly dressed, who spoke confidently at meetings and was entirely devoted to the socialist feminist and suffragist cause and then to Christian Science, is all there is. The writers do not even hint at any early heterosexual romance, the usual practice to establish single women's "normal" sexual credentials. Yet they do allude to the 'particular' friendship, the 'special companionship', she enjoyed with Cecilia John (better known to her friends as Celie) during the years of activism that took in the 1914–18 war.[25]

The two women were nominated in 1917 to represent the WPA and the Women's Peace Army at the International Women's Peace Conference to be held in Europe when the war ended. They sailed in March 1919. After an adventurous trip involving several delays, they arrived to find the conference venue had been changed from Paris to Zurich, in neutral Switzerland. They eventually reached the conference, after which the two made their way to London via Paris in short stages, staying in hotels and sight-seeing. There they parted company, both 'bitterly disillusioned with conventional politics'. Celie returned to Australia via America while Vida remained in England for the next three years.[26]

The WPA disbanded in 1919 while Vida Goldstein and Cecilia John were in Europe attending the Women's Peace Conference. When Vida returned to Australia in 1923, then aged fifty-three, she immersed herself completely in Christian Science with the same zeal she had brought to politics. She lived with her sisters in the Melbourne suburb of South Yarra until her death in 1949. She did visit London again in 1929 with her sister Mrs Hyde Champion, meeting up with Mary Fullerton and Mabel Singleton at the latter's office in Kensington: 'First an all round yabber then we went to the cinema Cafe near by and had dinner then to a show, a Silent followed by a talkie'.[27] Mary and Mabel were not enamoured of Christian Science, Mabel confessing after Vida's death to a 'feeling of disappointment through the years that she should have taken such a step'.[28]

Cecilia John finally settled in England, returning there around 1924, possibly via European war relief work. I do not know if she and Vida Goldstein remained friends, although it *was* Celie who notified Mabel that Vida and her sister were in London in 1929. In a letter from Mary to her sisters in Australia, she records that she and Mabel spent Christmas 1925 'with Celie John and her adopted child Vasitchsky'.[29] There is no later mention of this 'child', although there is reference to a female 'partner' in a detailed account Mary gave of a visit on Boxing Day 1929 to Celie's 300-year-old country cottage in Surrey. Celie drove Mary, Mabel, her son Denis, and Mabel's secretary Jean Hamilton, to the cottage in her car. Mary describes the cottage and garden, telling her sisters that Celie 'and her partner, Miss Driver, go there for weekends all the year round, the car of course making that possible'.[30] In 1992, Denis Singleton told me he recalled many visits he had made with his mother and Mary to that country cottage with Celie and 'her friend', whose name he remembers only as Elizabeth.

Mary described Cecilia John as 'a goer' whose restoration of her dilapidated cottage's sagging ceilings and covered-up oak beams was an undertaking 'no one but she would have had the courage to tackle'. During the years of political activity with the WPA, Celie John and Mabel Singleton often featured in newspaper reports as physically strong and courageous women. On one occasion, Mabel had to shout above the din of a dissenting crowd to declare a meeting of Vida's closed; on another, Celie turned a fire hose on a soldier who tried to grab the WPA flag from her. At a riot at the Bijou Theatre in December 1915, after Celie had sung the banned peace song, 'I Didn't Raise My Son To Be a Soldier' to loud boos and stamping feet, she and Mabel jumped onto to the platform to protect the speaker, Adela Pankhurst, one standing on each side of the diminutive woman as soldiers rushed the stage.[31]

In later years these two women continued to share similar interests in London. Mabel had done a physical training course in Melbourne and Celie John became a teacher in the Dalcrose system of Eurythmic dancing, an interest Mabel shared. (Mary was glad they could accompany each other to displays of what she called 'Greek dancing', as she found the dancing graceful but boring after a time). In August 1924, Celie joined Mabel, Mary and Denis on a trip to Ehrwald in Austria to take part in a Summer School 'on a system of Breathing Culture', called the 'Bret Harte system', the serious participants being the two who were interested in physical culture.[32] These two women inspired mythical comparisons among their friends: Vida once described Celie as a 'Titan', while Miles Franklin compared Mabel to 'Boadicea' and 'Britannia'. It is perhaps fitting that both these Amazonian women, at different sessions of the WPA Women's Parliament, were elected by their peers to the office of Prime Minister.

As I became absorbed in the pages of *Woman Voter*, I found the accounts of life in the WPA so indicative of a lively female-centred society that comparisons with the women's liberation movement sixty to seventy years later inevitably sprang to my mind. Australian historian, Pat Gowland, believes that the Women's Peace Army and the Women's Political Association 'did evolve some form of feminist separatism' and that 'their consciousness of the concept of "sisterhood" may have been unique up until that time and is a forerunner of the second-wave feminist concept of "woman-identified woman"'.[33] One of the major differences between the two "waves" of feminism cannot be ignored however. Constructions of sexuality had changed to such an extent by the 1970s and '80s that it was possible for a self-conscious lesbian politics to be part of the agenda. And that politics was integral to the concept of woman-identification.

Adrienne Rich, one of its main proponents, placed all women on a 'lesbian continuum', arguing for it as a natural state which the institution of compulsory heterosexuality forces women to reject.[34] Friendship in this version, ironically, becomes absorbed into an all-encompassing but non-specific lesbianism. Rich's concept of the lesbian continuum, though ground-breaking, was ahistorical and essentialist in that it did not take into account the changing constructions and understandings of sexual categories.

Writing around the same time, Lillian Faderman explored centuries of women's friendships, providing a linear historical view of lesbianism. Her theoretical construction of "romantic friendship" describes a tradition of condoned female friendships over several centuries, destroyed at the end of the nineteenth century by the sexologists' categorising of the "lesbian" as an abnormal, masculine woman who inverted normal femininity. The problem with this linear model of friendship is that it depends on the notion of historical progress – "now" is better than "then" – which can lead to unintended condescension on the part of the historian. Faderman asks rhetorically why women 'accepted and internalized' the views of the sexologists and answers with this conjecture: 'Perhaps because to resist would have taken more self-confidence than fledgling full human beings (which women were just becoming around the turn of the century) could muster'.[35] Such high-handed evolutionary politics reads over the top of all the strategies and devices that women like Mary Fullerton and her colleagues at the Women's Political Association did deploy in order to create a cultural space for themselves in the early twentieth century.

Feminists of the 1970s and '80s had a considerable investment in the paradigm of women's 'identification' because it enabled them to propose an alternative, relational way of operating in the world. Teresa de Lauretis points to the deficiencies of this model in conceptualising desire between women, observing that 'the sweeping of lesbian sexuality and desire under the rug of sisterhood, female friendship, and the now popular theme of the mother-daughter bond, has become canonical in feminist criticism . . . In all three parts of the rug, what is in question is not desire, but identification'.[36] It seems to me that the collapse of desire into identification is the greatest limitation of the model of woman-orientation. Sameness is revered, difference ignored. The only difference recognised is the sexual difference between male and female. But what about difference within the category "woman"? Isn't that part of what creates lesbian desire?

One of the most productive tensions in Mary Fullerton's love poetry is that between identification and separateness, between affinity and difference. Her life was almost completely woman-centred, but identification was not the only thing she sought in a soul-mate, as her 1904 poem 'The Complement' indicated. She desired a lover who would complement her, not one who would be her identical twin. Mary perceived her relationship with Mabel to be a friendship and she did not consider herself to be an 'invert' or even a 'Sapphist'. Yet in that sketch called 'The Justification', written in 1903 before she met Mabel, about 'one of those women who love individuals of their own sex with all the intensity with which most women love individuals of the opposite sex', she contended that 'essential differences heat the furnace of passion'.[37] For the flame to continue, a deeper affinity was required. And the recognition of difference, not identification, was the vital spark.

The model of romantic friendship that was applied by the lesbian feminists of the 1970s is able to account for some aspects of the relationship between Mary Fullerton and Mabel Singleton, while the homosocial world of the WPA certainly appears to have been one in which such friendships could flourish. But these dimensions cannot deal with the desire that is expressed in the love poems and which differentiated this relationship from, say, Mary's friendship with Miles Franklin. Desire is the force propelling the love poetry that flowed from Mary Fullerton's pen, the mysterious 'thing' evoked in the 1917 poem Mary wrote for Mabel, 'Your Nib's First Task':

> This golden nib shall surely write
> The golden word, the golden word
> And somehow to your sense translate

That which is neither seen [n]or heard.

The thing evading speech or script;
In golden form, in golden form
Will spill itself upon my page
A spirit iridescent, warm.

The Being of my love expressed
A precious thing, not read but known
A magic message for the Soul
Of you alone, for you alone.

POETRY AND DESIRE

Some Australian feminists have condemned these women as "wowsers" (an Australian term of unknown origin meaning prudish or puritanical), but it needs to be remembered that women then had few rights to sexual autonomy. The feminists in the Women's Political Association followed what is sometimes known today as a politics of purity, arguing that the unlimited access men had to women's bodies made equality in sex relations impossible. Contraception was inadequate and unreliable, abortion illegal and dangerous, and men's conjugal rights were sacrosanct. The idea that women could claim marital rape, for instance, would have been unthinkable. In addition, venereal disease was rife, and feminists fought long and hard to insist that men take responsibility for their sexual behaviour.

The WPA held a Women's Convention from May to June 1916. Its purpose was to advocate measures to combat what they called 'The Social Evil', that is, sexually transmitted disease. The convention was attended by women from a wide range of organisations, including political groups, religious groups, district councils and trade unions. It argued for 'a twin policy of prevention and cure', one in which education was emphasised. On 19 June 'Miss Fullerton moved, Mrs Singleton seconded: That this Convention demands an equal moral standard for men and women – and that, the highest'.[1] Mary argued that there were two different moral standards in civilised life, and that part of the 'sex privilege' man had allowed himself involved the degradation of women, particularly in prostitution.

Given the feminist politics followed by these activist women of first-wave feminism, it was unlikely they condoned any form of sexual libertarianism, whether heterosexual free love or same-sex Sapphism. Many took the line that love relationships between women and men were not possible on an equal basis, that even in marriage (which was the only choice for respectable women to follow) they were exploited as wives and mothers. Of the three women we are concerned with here, Mabel Singleton had a short and unhappy marriage, Miles Franklin adopted a stance of heterosexual celibacy, while Mary Fullerton always maintained she lacked what she called the sex instinct.

Sex in all of Mary's writings is both explicitly and implicitly defined in terms of heterosexuality. With reference to the lack of sex instinct, she once explained to Miles that she was 'born so – that is that the process of reproduction is repulsive to me'.[2] The 'process' she referred to involved both the act of heterosexual intercourse and motherhood; female sexual desire and maternal instinct were strongly linked in understandings of female sexuality at the time. Mary Fullerton always claimed she had neither sexual interest in the opposite sex nor desire to be a mother. But when she disputed society's disparagement of 'go alone' women in her memoirs, she was also suggesting that to lack the so-called sex instinct did not mean an inability to feel emotion: '"Unwomanly", "cold-hearted", and so forth, are the charges levelled. I have heard these words and their like applied to myself. I have smiled, knowing them to be from an entirely false understanding of me'.[3]

With knowledge of Mary's writings about her love for Mabel Singleton, a subtext to this statement emerges; so also does the writer's need to find an identity, or subject position, for herself that did not define her as abnormal, as the lesbian discourse of the time would undoubtedly have done. To do this she had to remain "asexual". But I believe she was able to create a space for her same-sex desire, and that she found that space within the framework of a transcendental vision of friendship based, unlikely as it may seem, on the writings of nineteenth-century American philosopher, Ralph Waldo Emerson.

The conception of friendship she was to develop was highly influenced by this philosopher and poet, whose writing she discovered long after her study sessions in the wash house at Glenmaggie. In 'Memoirs' she recalls the importance of 'the influence of Emerson and his Transcendentalism: I read eagerly a philosopher to my taste. I realize in looking back that the indefinite appeals to me much more than the cut and dried – the dogmatic. There is a fine, large suggestiveness about the early American seer. His "over-soul" how much more palatable than the thundering God with his anathemas'.[4]

Mary always recognised, and indeed, celebrated ambiguity in religion and in other areas of life. The appeal of the 'indefinite' was a crucial factor in her ability to forge a space for herself, one that could accommodate her love for women, within what we might call mainstream ways of thinking. Emerson's metaphysical conception of the 'over-soul' – a spiritual governing force that existed not only in the outer world but also within the individual soul – offered a freedom to act and take control over one's destiny that was denied in more orthodox Christian accounts such as the Presbyterianism that was central to her upbringing.

Emerson's essay 'Friendship', published in the 1860s, provides at least one of the intellectual sources of what I perceive to be Mary's construction of same-sex desire, that is, the productive tension between sameness and difference, affinity and separateness. He describes the productive interplay of friendship and solitude thus: 'The soul environs itself with friends, that it may enter into a grander self-acquaintance or solitude; and it goes alone for a season, that it may exalt its conversation or society'.[5] Mary described herself as a 'go alone' woman. Yet in her unpublished poetry, even before she met Mabel Singleton, there is a consistent fantasy that somewhere there existed a soul-mate, a woman whose complementarity was Mary's destiny.

The model for a form of friendship that could sustain such a fantasy also appears in Emerson's essay, for he conceived the more commonly considered 'social benefit' of friendship to be subordinate to the 'select and sacred relation' that was friendship in its highest form: 'The higher the style we demand of friendship, of course the less easy to establish it with flesh and blood. We walk alone in the world. Friends, such as we desire, are dreams and fables. But a sublime hope cheers the ever-faithful heart, that elsewhere, in other regions of the universal power, souls are now acting, enduring, and daring which can love us and which we can love'.[6]

I believe it is significant that it was a man's and not a woman's model of friendship that proved to be so influential upon Mary Fullerton. Although Emerson does not gender his discussion of friendship, the unstated dynamic is undoubtedly one of male fraternity. He conceived friendship not simply as the supportive nurturing relationship commonly considered to be experienced by women, but as one that required the 'roughest courage', a challenging relationship based on difference as well as similarity or identification.

Mary Fullerton seems to have adapted Emerson's "masculine" version of friendship to her own lived experience as a woman. Through her chosen medium of poetry, she incorporated this blend of theory and experience into her attempts to articulate her own sexual desire. The result was not derived from the sexologists' understanding of the woman-loving woman as "like a man"; it also circumvented both the conflation of lesbian desire with the nurturing, non-sexual mother/daughter bond, and female desire in general with maternal instinct. I use the term 'sexual' in spite of Mary's professed lack of 'sex instinct', according to the way Teresa de Lauretis has defined lesbian desire, as a concept that includes centrally 'the conscious presence of desire in one woman for another'. In this understanding, 'it is that desire, rather than woman-identification or even the sexual act itself . . . that specifies lesbian sexuality'.[7] Sameness and difference are both implicated here: the lure of identification is as crucial a component as the frisson of difference. Their juxtaposition is what creates lesbian desire.

In her published poetry, Mary Fullerton often reiterates the theme of separateness. With her characteristic love of paradox, she elucidates it most clearly in 'Lovers':

> To be unloved brings sweet relief:
> The strong adoring eyes
> Play the eternal thief
> With the soul's fit disguise.

> He will not sleep, and let be drawn
> The screen of thy soul's ark;
> They keep, those lidless eyes,
> Thy sanctuary stark.
>
> God, when he made each separate
> Unfashioned to his own act,
> Giving the lover eyes,
> So his love's soul be sacked.
>
> To be unloved brings sweet relief;
> The one integrity
> Of soul is to be lone,
> Inviolate, and free.[8]

The sentiments expressed in 'Lovers' echo Emerson's belief that the soul needs to go 'alone for a season' in order to reaffirm its separateness. The poem's title and the poet's struggle to resist the power of the lover's 'strong adoring eyes' implies that that separation from the lover requires a supreme effort of will.

Many of the poems Mary wrote for Mabel Singleton emphasise the desire for affinity, recalling another Emersonian dynamic: the dream of a 'select and sacred' form of friendship. Sometimes that dream seems a reality to the poet, as in the poem Mary wrote for Mabel's birthday, 'September 9th, 1912', the typescript of which has two sets of initials handwritten at the bottom of the page: M.E.S. and M.E.F. It begins:

> The years are three according to man's measurement
>   Since first we met, since first we met;
> Since, many suns from out the firmament,
>   And many moons have set.
> And many many more shall climb and fall
>   *Ere I forget*
>
> Doom, and the days may jar and harass me
>   Without an end, without an end,
> But I shall never break though I be pressed,
>   Because of what the gods did send,
> With rue and balm from the Invisible
>   *My friend, my friend*

It is tempting, isn't it, to read Mary's oscillation between separateness and affinity as her public and private versions of her love for Mabel Singleton? We could then consider the private, unpublished poetry to be the truer picture. But then we would be reducing her to a closeted lesbian who maintained a public stance of asexuality while leading a secret love-life with her female companion. While considerations of privacy and the lack of any positive lesbian narrative to draw from are no doubt implicated in Mary's construction and playing out of her sexual identity, that's not the whole story. Read in conjunction with each other, Mary Fullerton's poems establish a complex dynamic, one that incorporates the lesbian lure of sameness *and* the necessity to maintain a separate identity.

Mary wrote a poem called 'In Solitude' in 1913, in the very early years of the two women's relationship when they were staying at the home of Mabel's family in Walsall, England. Here, the poet's enforced solitude in her separate bedroom is made wonderful by the 'presence' of her friend. It suggests, perhaps, that although they cannot openly share the same room, they are at least together and not parted as they were in their separate homes in Australia. The first line quotes (or actually misquotes a line from a Wordsworth sonnet):

> "Nuns fret not at their narrow cells."
> Nor I forsooth at mine,
> Since in my solitude I had
> A presence such as thine.
> Who could feel exiled on such terms
> Be downcast, or repine?
>
> Not I beloved, immediate friend,
> The chosen of my heart,
> Glad in thy presence, and unstrung
> When we alas must part
> So dear – unspeakably dear
> Thou wert, will be, and art.

In 'Withdrawal', written many years later and published posthumously, Mary refers directly to the problem of merging, a term that has acquired currency in contemporary psychological literature about lesbian relationships, where the individual's separate identity is in danger of being lost. Although this poem was published four years after the collection in which 'Lovers' appears, the concerns of the two poems are so similar they may have been written around the same time, as the poems in both *Moles Do So Little With Their Privacy* and *The Wonder and the Apple* were drawn from the large pool sent by Mary to her friend, Miles Franklin. 'Withdrawal' begins with the lines:

> To be together is not all:
> Between me and your smile
> A little while
> I must put up a wall.

Later the poet reminds her lover that

> Time's units are not made to blend:
> Though love be very sweet
> It is not meet
> That friend should merge in friend.

'Withdrawal' concludes with a return to the image of the 'wall', but with the difference that both lovers must strive to maintain their separateness in the face of love's allure:

> Togetherness must not be all:
> Between love and love's smile
> A little while
> We must put up the wall.[9]

Compare the sentiments of 'Withdrawal', in which the poet must shield herself against her lover's smile, with a poem written many years earlier, long before thoughts of merging were an issue and when love's 'smile' was just an erotic dream:

> Flash to me half a glance
>   The wraith of a smile
> So I fold it safe in my heart
>   For the afterwhile
> . . .
> Hearts must have food for life
>   And wine for the dream
> Ah! flash me the wraith of a smile
>   That a kiss shall seem.[10]

Meaning in poetry is relational. It involves the rational mind, the imagination, the emotions and the senses as it is experienced visually, aurally and intellectually; even the most basic experience of living – breathing – is an integral part of it. Poetry is very much an embodied experience. What better medium for exploring desire ('the thing evading speech or script') than a type of script that itself evades prescriptive readings. Through her poetry, Mary played out the evolving complexities of her relationship with the woman she met in 1909 at the age of forty-one and with whom she shared the rest of her life. She seems to have worked towards transforming the Emersonian vision of a form of friendship that exists 'in other regions of the universal power' into an actuality that could exist in the here and now, and between two *women*.

Mary's love poems to Mabel privilege the soul over the senses, love or spiritual affinity over sexual desire; but soul and sense, affinity and desire are constantly implicated with each other in the practice of the poetry. The erotic language of the body permeates her work through her verbs rather than her visual imagery. Her lovers strive for a perfect union of souls, but at the same time their bodies pulse, throb, breathe, blossom, spill and flow, either literally or metaphorically.

One image that Mary uses repeatedly in her poems to Mabel is that of the violet, which, in her work, always stands for a powerful female sensuality. This image has a history of women-loving associations dating back to Sappho, who wrote of the violet tiaras she and her lovers wore in their hair. In one untitled sonnet, Mary writes:

> You say that violets fade upon your breast,
> I'd rather dearest that mine perished there
> Quick on your passionate heart than otherwhere.
> Did some cold vase become their purpled nest
> They longer there might live to die unblest:
> Better their fragrance float about your hair,
> Your heart-beats pulse their sweetness to the air
> That breathed again gives aromatic rest.
>
> The flower was made to give to Beauty dreams,
> And when its soul for her behoof is spilled
> So hers be fed by transitory gleams

With Meanings clear, its mission is fulfilled.
Breathing of love in its suspiring breath
Let the flower swoon to its luxurious death.

Here the poet *becomes* the violets she desires to place on her lover's breast in a fantasy of erotic exchange: 'Better their fragrance float about your hair,/Your heart-beats pulse their sweetness to the air/ That breathed again gives aromatic rest'. The whole movement of this poem suggests the process of love-making, culminating in the flower's 'swoon to a luxurious death' reminiscent of *la petite mort,* 'the little death' of sexual climax.

Mary Fullerton's unwavering commitment to feminism coincided with a strong homosocial disposition. I believe that her unpublished poetry to her friend enacts a desire that was not only homosocial but also homoerotic or "lesbian", even though she perceived her relationship with Mabel to be a friendship. The separateness of being that she aspired to did not necessarily clash with her fantasy of affinity with another woman because this did not involve the subordination she believed to be implicit in male/female relationships. The affinity that she sought was one of complementarity rather than absorption into the other person, for she was aware of the 'essential differences' necessary for desire to exist. Women are socially constructed as relational, as nurturant and caring beings who put others' needs first. So the balance needed to maintain a productive affinity, one that allows the individual to retain her separateness and yet make the exchange of desire possible, is not easy to maintain. Mary had to constantly redraw the boundary between herself and her friend in her poetry. The tension between sameness and difference, between affinity and separateness in relationships between women renders their status precarious and shifting, but that same productive tension can also be part of what constitutes lesbian desire.

A CHILD IS BORN

M ary Fullerton became Acting President of the WPA in early 1911 while Vida Goldstein was travelling in England 'to help the women's cause at the heart of the action'.[1] At the Annual General Meeting held in March that year, Mary (Vice President) and Mabel (Secretary) were among the office-bearers who were re-elected unopposed. A letter from 'Mrs Singleton' was read out at this meeting, 'thanking the Association for granting her continual leave of absence and expressing her determination to take, in the near future, the same active part in the work as she had done in the past'.[2]

At that time, Mabel Singleton was ensconced in a large timber house set amid 120 acres of bushland on Mount Dandenong, some fifty miles from Melbourne. She was there looking after her baby son, Denis Gordon Singleton, born two months earlier on 14 January. Muyanato was the holiday house belonging to Mabel's wealthy husband and, according to the story Denis himself was later told, he and his mother were 'banished' there directly after his birth at Haverbrack. Robert and Mabel Singleton never lived together again.

Three months before Mabel gave birth to her son, Mary (who had retreated to Glenmaggie) wrote a fierce poem called 'Won?'. In it, the poet rehearses a battle between 'Circumstance' and 'Fate' for the love of a woman 'of heroic mould' who is, I am sure, Mabel Singleton. Mary is clearly represented as Fate, Circumstance by a man who could be Mabel's husband, Robert Singleton. The poem begins:

> Can she condemned of Circumstance
> Endure the lover in his glance?
> She of heroic mould, but made
> To fit a modern masquerade.

Later, the poet bewails her position:

> Oh Fate o'erthrown by Circumstance,
> Is Destiny subdued by Chance?

> He woos; he stays; his vulgar ring
> Upon her hand is glittering.

'Won?' finally answers its own question with an allusion to the 'soul' of the poet's friend, which aligns her with Fate and not Circumstance:

> He shall not *win* her all those days
> That join their strange incongruous ways
> For Circumstance may *wed* like Fate
> But Circumstance can never *mate*.
> His ineffectual days shall run
> She never never shall be won;
> But only she shall know not he
> That his success is Tragedy.
> For in her eyes against his breast
> Shuddered repulsion and unrest
> Her soul one moment in those eyes
> Looked naked and without disguise
> Ere to his face she schooled her glance
> And gave herself to Circumstance.

Mary is here re-enacting the theory of complementary souls that underpins her construction of desire, where 'mating' takes on a dimension beyond its conventional, heterosexual meaning. According to this poem, 'Destiny' is not to be 'subdued by Chance', symbolised in the 'vulgar ring' that glitters on the woman's finger. The suggestion is that this woman will, through the guidance of her friend's love, cast off the 'masquerade', the loveless marriage she has been 'made to fit', and fulfil her destiny as 'woman soul'.

Mystery surrounds the birth of Denis Singleton and the subsequent separation of his parents. Denis's own explanation is that his father, who had already had six children from his former marriage, wanted no more and was furious when he was born. Robert Singleton was the owner of a considerable estate and there is suggestion in Mary Fullerton's poetry that she considered Mabel to have been swayed from the path of her destiny by money. 'Won?' refers to the man in it as a 'gilded clown' and the relationship as a 'masquerade'. Perhaps, as I suggested earlier, the marriage *did* contain some practical conditions for the young woman from the English industrial midlands, such as an embargo on children in return for a comfortable life in a far-off country. Denis Singleton's explanation is a possibility; after all, Robert Singleton was seventy years old at the time of his youngest son's birth. But the 'banishment' appears to be a decided over-reaction to a situation that was, presumably, partly of his own making.

Although he did acknowledge Denis as his son in his will, another possible explanation of Robert Singleton's extreme reaction is hard to ignore. Perhaps he knew he could not really have fathered the child, through abstinence or even impotence. Or perhaps he was physically absent around the time of conception. Was Mabel having an affair? Although the poem, 'Won?', seems to suggest that the poet is referring to her friend's marriage, it has an urgency about it that might be a reaction to her friend's pregnancy, but could also suggest that Mabel was involved with another man. Several other poems appear to support the explanation of a lover, though the fact that they are undated makes them even more problematic as "evidence" than the other poems. Four that appear to have been written together speak of the poet's loss of her friend's love. The last, 'The Portion', finishes:

> For you his voice, for me my own
> Flung backward in the wind,
> For me to speak his name alone
> In solitudes unkind?
> For him the glory of your eyes,
> For you his shielding hand;
> For me the loneliness that lies
> Outside Love's radiant land.

Another poem, 'Betrayed', which gives no clue to its possible date or connection with other poems, describes a parting and a birth:

> She heard a voice within her heart
> Pronounce the words "for ever",
> He drew her to his arms, and blent
> His echo to her word, and sent
> His eager vow to meet it;

And with her ear upon his breast
At once in passion and in rest,
She heard his heart repeat it.

They parted; and another word
Within her sense is droning
She clasps his infant in her arms
And soothes its innocent alarms
With that sad voice that ever
Within her heart its monotone
Goes pulsing on, its stifled groan
Its "never, never, never".

The first stanza of this poem resembles the last part of 'Won?' but with the marked difference that there is no duplicity on the part of the woman here. She is 'betrayed' in what sounds like a conventional narrative. The poem hints at a lover's desertion after sexual favours; it does not sound like an elderly husband's angry banishment of his wife.

Many years later, when Mary was near death and her friend was nursing her, Mabel wrote these cryptic words to Emily Fullerton, one of Mary's sisters: 'There's nothing "good" or "noble" about my care for Mary: it's one of those friendships that gives all. Some day I can tell you all how Mary saved me from *desperation* in those first days after we met'.[3] The word 'desperation' is underlined in the original letter. There is no record that she did ever tell that story, but it seems clear that Mabel Singleton's marriage was not happy long before the birth of her son.

While Mary Fullerton wrote angry and despairing poems about the father of Mabel's baby, she appears to have been unreservedly welcoming of the baby himself, even before his birth, something that could mitigate against the suggestion that she was ousted in her friend's affections by a lover. 'A Lullaby', written two weeks before the baby was born, begins:

I breathe a truth
    For the days to be,
When the cradle of Life
    Shall compass thee.

The poem goes on to tell the unborn baby that its mother has 'dreamed thee good' and 'willed thee sweet' even though 'Others may quarrel' and 'Others may frown'. Mary does not seem to blame her friend in any way for her pregnancy, which must have occurred around April 1910, just seven months after the joyful poems that record their coming together. And even around the time she wrote the angry poem, 'Won?', there is an untroubled, passionate sonnet to Mabel's beauty dated just a few days later. The whole episode remains an intriguing puzzle.

I don't know if Mary was present at the birth of Denis Singleton, but she certainly appears to have been at Mabel's side soon afterwards. On Denis's eighteenth birthday, Mary wrote to Miles Franklin that it 'seems a year only since I saw his little dark head beside his mother at Haverbrack Malvern Melbourne'.[4] I do not know, either, just how soon after the birth Mabel and her baby were 'banished' to Muyanato on Mount Dandenong, but by early June 1911, Mary was staying there with them, writing poems of contrasting moods to her lover.

The poetry Mary wrote to Mabel in the early years of their relationship often follows a pattern of rapturous lyrical poems interspersed with others which berate her friend for being cold and unfeeling, usually followed by a swift change of mood in which she begs her lover for forgiveness. Mary was something of a bowerbird when it came to writing these expressions of her feelings; she often modelled poems that were never intended for publication on borrowings from her wide reading. The deliriously erotic 'Why Did You Sleep?', written on 4 June, is clearly inspired by the work of the 19th-century English poet Christina Rossetti, whom Mary admired:

> Why did I sleep? Because an Elfin time
> Went sounding through the grottos of my heart;
> And floating down my spirit's avenue a rune
> That Fairyland might sigh for when her moon
> Melts on her vales, and her musicians start
> Their symphonies and all the flower lips part
> And every grass blade is a harpstring soon
> Transcending all the ecstasies of Art.
>
> Ah sweeter far the Elfin song that sang
> Me first to sleep with languid serenade

> Then in my dreams its mellow echoes rang
> And a soft Paradise my Night Land made;
> So all the night vibrating still I heard
> In gulfs of warm perfume your parting word.

Only a few days later, on the 10th, she wrote 'The Hero of Loedsley Hall to His Lady' (the title being a reference to a Tennyson poem), in which the berating and pleas for forgiveness occur:

> I cut delib'rately in marble verse
> Cold, set, and fourteen-lined, my marble mood
> Of chill antipathy. I see your nature rude
> Your callous heartlessness – and worse;
> You marble beauty that I did universe
> In glowing Idealism! Ah how could
> Love by you passionless be understood?
> You smooth-cheeked statue I that love you, curse.
>
> . . . My purpose falters . . . and I cannot cut
> Or chisel anger for I feel the heart
> Of tender pulsing life, and the heart shut
> Is opened to me . . . I am at your feet,
> Crying your living spirit "make me live".
> Crying your loving heart "forgive, forgive".

There also remain from this time tender poems to Denis, such as the lullaby 'Baby's Moon' written on 9 June, the last part of which reads:

> Moon is the baby's
>   He is his mother's
> Moon guard them both for
>   Each is the other's.

A more sanguine view of this turbulent time, written from the point of view of colleagues who were not privy to the emotional upheavals occurring at Muyanato, appears in the pages of *Woman Voter* for 1 June 1911 (indicating that Mary had joined Mabel some time before the month of June). An article written by two of the WPA members describes a trip they had just made to Mount Dandenong to visit their friends. The writers inform the members that their Acting President, Mary Fullerton, is at Mrs Singleton's home taking 'a much-needed time of rest, made necessary partly by her strenuous efforts on behalf of our association'. The story starts in the small mountain town of Sassafras (to which they would have travelled from the city by train), where they hire an open four-wheeled trap drawn by 'a pair of sturdy country ponies' to take them the rest of the way to Mount Dandenong. It proved an arduous journey. The ascent of Mount Dandenong itself took an hour and a half among falling snowflakes 'which quickly powdered hair and face or found a resting-place where fur collar and neck meet'.

Their enthusiasm undampened, the women finally reached Muyanato where, after tea and toast in front of a blazing log fire with Mabel and Mary, they indulged in 'a crowded hour of glorious talk'. Leaving at three o'clock, they made their return journey 'in brilliant sunshine'. Oddly enough, this little vignette makes no mention of Mabel Singleton's baby. Perhaps the visitors did not feel this was necessary, since Denis had been present at a WPA meeting in March at which he and another infant (named Vida Mabel Mary Breden after the WPA leaders) were made life members of the association. It was recorded in *Woman Voter* that 'the children took evident interest in the proceedings'.[5]

When Mary left Muyanato to return to Melbourne on 13 July, she wrote 'Life's Scented Manuscript (Omar) (Altered)', a poem which indicates how important in her life were both mother and child:

> A scented precious page
>   – I turn it down
> And sadly set my face away
>   Toward the town.
>
> But there shall be no seal
>   Upon that page,
> Nor can its clinging scent give place
>   To yellowed age.
>
> Nor can old Time efface
>   What there is writ,
> Nor steal the sweet ambrosial dreams
>   That flow from it.
>
> For it breathes all things fair
>   That Life has sent;
> Of *Him* and *You*, of *You* and *Him*
>   Is redolent.

While continuing to work long hours for the WPA as well as trying to earn a living as a journalist, Mary Fullerton made frequent trips to Mount Dandenong from Hawthorn to be with the two people who were central to her existence. She was at Muyanato again in September 1911, where she wrote a letter to Marie Pitt, a fellow poet in Melbourne who also came from Gippsland. After apologising to 'Mrs Pitt' for not having written to the Gippsland papers as promised about her poems because of her 'unsatisfactory state of health', Mary finishes her letter with a statement, the formality of which cannot disguise its underlying emotional content. She says she is 'happily circumstanced . . . "where it smiles". The wide expanse of lower world and splendid background of Mountain bush constitutes an inanimate not to be bettered, and my dear friends Mother and Son a foreground centre and background of the human element – the animate which says the last word'.[6]

Mary's poems indicate that the two women and baby Denis spent about a month holidaying at Newhaven on Phillip Island near Melbourne a few months later, in March 1912. Once again the leave-taking was painful, as indicated by the sonnet of 26 March, written in pencil and simply called 'Parting'. Like 'Why Did You Sleep?', its erotic undertones are unmistakable:

> A little shadow made the waters grey
> This morning when I saw them from the beach;
> And all along the cliff the ocean's speech
> Was in a minor tone, and all the way
> Returning too, though gracious was the day
> Full of sun arrows through the oval reach
> From East to West; and on the waters lay
> The bright boon of reflection from [? illegible].
>
> And so I mused, and found the monotone
> The grey were not in sea or shafted sky
> No pink whorled shell did iterate the moan,
> No sighing wave caught murmurous reply.
> Oh friend! Knowest thou the shadow and the grey
> The spiritual clime that wraps the parting day?

A poem hastily written on the back of an envelope in June of that year, when Mary dropped in and found her friend not at home, suggests that Mabel was no longer living on Mount Dandenong. The envelope on which the poem is written is addressed to Mrs Singleton, has Haverbrack crossed out and replaced by an address in South Yarra, an inner suburb of Melbourne where Mabel subsequently lived for several years.

One more extraordinary event surrounding Denis's birth and the demise of the Singleton marriage remains. On 26 June 1912, Mary, Mabel and Denis sailed for England on the *Orvieto*. The WPA held a farewell for the two stalwart members at the Austral Salon, but the report in *Woman Voter* made no mention of a planned return date. On 27 June 1912, just one day after the two women and baby had left, Robert Singleton made a new will, virtually disinheriting his estranged wife. In this last will, he appointed Stanley Robert Singleton, his 33-year-old eldest son from his first marriage, as his executor, and left him real estate and personal property valued at just under 14,000 pounds at the time of his death. Out of that, the will stipulated that a mere 200 pounds should go to Mabel Singleton, plus 800 pounds for Denis's education and maintenance. The other two surviving children from his first marriage fared somewhat better, receiving property and money to the value of 2000 pounds each.

Denis Singleton knows very little about the man to whom his mother was married. At my first meeting with him in London, he offered the matter-of-fact observation that Robert Singleton was a 'brute'. He said his father was never spoken of during his childhood, nor was he shown any photographs of him. When I met Denis again two years later, he repeated the story that his father had been 'livid' at his birth and had 'banished' his mother and himself from his life. He also commented that he thought his mother might have committed suicide after the flight to Muyanato had Mary not been there to support her. And he always felt his father was a taboo subject in the household where he grew up.

What is apparent from the fragments that I have been able to piece together of this intriguing story, puzzling and contradictory though some of them are, is that Mary Fullerton shared some involvement in the birth of her friend's son. Her relationship with

Mabel seems also to have been a factor in Robert Singleton's subsequent wrath and his disinheritance of his wife after the two women left for England.

Muyanato, where so much of this part of the story was played out, was eventually destroyed in one of the bushfires that periodically sweep through the Dandenong Ranges. Haverbrack, the Singleton mansion in Malvern, was demolished in 1935, an event commemorated in an article in the Melbourne magazine, *Table Talk*. [7] Stanley Singleton, who owned Haverbrack up to its demise, was interviewed for the article and offers an inaccurate and rather romanticised history of the house and the Singleton family. No mention is made of Robert Singleton's second marriage; it is as if Mabel Singleton and her son Denis never existed.

TO ENGLAND AND BACK

M ary wrote a communal letter to her family in Melbourne and Gippsland when she and Mabel arrived in England in the summer of 1912 after more than five weeks at sea. A copy of part of this letter survives in the National Library in Canberra, the copy that was sent by her sisters in Melbourne to the Gippsland branch of the family.[1] There are four typescript pages, a fifth copied by hand on the back. The sister who has copied that part of Mary's letter, either Soph or Bell, explains that Em has typed most of it and that they will send the rest on if she gets round to typing it up. In the handwritten fragment, Mary describes how she had been suffering with a cold before they docked in London as a reaction to travelling through 'the tropics': 'So seedy was I that the last two days before landing I was dead weight and Mrs Singleton had to do my packing as well as her own'. This section of the letter also describes her meeting with Mabel's father, who she said 'is very like Mrs S. the olive complexion and a very young-looking man for over 70'.

The typed section of the letter is full of rapturous descriptions of her surroundings as Mary Fullerton tries to bring to life for her family the excitement of seeing England for the first time. For her English mother it would have brought back memories, but Mary was the first of the Fullerton children to visit the land Anglo-Australians commonly referred to as "home". The London docks were seen through 'grey misty rain', but Mary had been up at 5.30 a.m. for her first glimpse of the country through the porthole. Plymouth was what she saw and she told her sisters, 'if you want to know what I thought look up a certain passage of rhapsody in the first portion of Aurora Leigh when she returns to England'. Mary then provides her own version of the landscape at length, describing 'the tinted peaks', the 'small nooks of glorious greens of every shade', finishing: 'it made me fall in love with England at once'.

The *Orvieto* docked at Tilbury on the Thames at 7 a.m. and the women were met by relatives of both families. Mary's Suffolk cousin, Mary Sims, and a Mrs Gilbert were there to welcome her as well as Mabel's brother, Ralph, and her father and stepmother. The meeting with Mary Sims was brief. Promises were made to visit Suffolk and then the two women and baby were whisked straight off to Dover where Mabel's brother had taken a cottage for them for six weeks at St Margaret's Bay, 'as London is undesirable at this time of the year, and this is nicer than Walsall'.

Dr Ralph Jupp was a wealthy and influential man who had been a surgeon in the Boer War and who was later to be involved in the setting up of the film industry in Britain. The party left for Dover in the motor he had provided; 'a beauty it simply flies, holds six besides the driver', wrote the awestruck Mary. As the motor 'flew at thirty miles an hour', she describes the 'silvan beauty' of the landscape, the 'harvests ripe', 'mown hay scented and sweet', 'poppies in the corn and the familiar mangel wurzel'. She becomes almost incoherent as literary allusions come flooding into her mind (Em's almost complete lack of punctuation doesn't help): 'stories of Hardies [sic] Tess hoeing in the turnip field, the fat boy of Dingley Dell Canterbury pilgrims, Dan Chaucer The white dear cliffs of Dover, a thousand things of romance and history of memory and imagination'. And never far from her thoughts were the people she was sharing the experience with: 'Crowded in with the flying actuality, all the time the thought and this is England was with me, almost a dream but real enough with Denis sitting quiet with surprise on his mother's knee and she looking very happy with her brother beside her and a warm welcome ahead at the bungalow'.

The cottage Dr Jupp had rented was located about half a mile from the village of St Margaret's, 'within twenty feet of the tide'. Behind it loomed 'a chalk cliff fifty or sixty feet high'. The 'Bay Bungalow' itself was quaint and romantic: 'a charmingly old fashioned one bedroom' with 'a low ceiling in one part and going eccentrically high at another'. The last house of a scattered group along the bay overlooking the English Channel, the delighted visitors were able to see the French coast clearly, with 'always a number of ships dotted about the channel'.

The two women saw Mabel's brother off on the train back to

London the next morning and then his driver took them sight-seeing to Canterbury in the motor that had been left for their convenience. The driver and a 'youth in Doctor R's employ' who was provided 'to help in odd ways with Denis etc' presumably stayed in separate lodgings or the one-bedroom cottage would have been very crowded.

Mary wrote many loving poems to her friend during this idyll by the sea; it seems to have provided a space for them both to recover from a turbulent two years. Denis's birth and the break-up of the Singleton marriage had caused extremes of both joy and distress for Mabel and, in a different way, for her devoted friend. These pressures, combined with the constant and strenuous political work for the WPA, had also imposed an increasing strain on Mary's already fragile physical health. 'You', which Mary wrote on 15 August, is first of the St Margaret's Bay poems: 'Now after many days of land and sea / A whispering spirit prompts my hand to write'. As usual, the poet seems to have had no difficulty searching her mind for a theme:

> Mine roams not farther than this beach tonight
> Glad prisoner of the chalk cliff guardian's white
> I lie and hear the waves' soft ministry.
>
> Their rhythm gives my theme and my content
> And so I know glad prisoner in this pebbly nook
> Why mind and heart no farther wanderings took
> But with the shore's soft voice their murmurs blent
> Because these voices say one name the while they dream
> Ah need I tell it now – their whisper and my theme?

Another poem – 'written at 7.30 pm. 12 Sept., 1912. At the Bay Bungalow – St Margaret's Bay', untitled and dedicated '*To You*' – is in elegiac mood, melancholy yet suffused with a stillness and peace that suggests a process of recovery after great stress. Throughout her life, the Australian writer who grew up in the inland heart of Victoria appears to have found strength and solace in the sea:

> The moving tents upon the waters go,
> The beacons blossom out like evening eyes;
> Near me is gloom, and mystic lights afar,

> Where through the grey the cliffs of France arise
> – Pale spectral cliffs – pale as moon pictures are,
> And as beneath the moon our wan world lies.

The final verse reiterates the poet's belief in her power to provide the loving support for her friend that would be able to save them both:

> Oh love! as [comes?] the haven to the sail
> Long weary of salt winds and hectoring seas;
> Within the calm but passioned love I give
> Find thou thy rest from Life's complexities
> Lean thou thy heart; and gather strength to live
> So thou and I fulfil our destinies.

A year later, back in Melbourne, Mary was to recall the time the lovers spent at St Margaret's Bay in Mabel's birthday poem for 'September 9th, 1913':

> Oh love: out of the here and now
>   Last year remember;
> The cliff's white-fronted brow
>   In chill September.
>
> . . .
>
> Oh love, under the chalky cliff
>   Your nest below;
> Someone was loving you
>   In the old bungalow.
>
> Dear love back in the now and here,
>   This truth remember;
> You are to me as dear,
>   As last September.

Over the coming year, both women were to find great need of the strength they had gathered during their sojourn at St Margaret's Bay. With Denis, they spent the Christmas/New Year period at Mabel's family home at Walsall, near Birmingham. There, it seems, Mabel's love for her little son was rekindled. In 'Exiled', written on the last day of 1912, Mary speaks of a reconciliation between mother and child, as if Mabel had been so withdrawn as to seem 'absent':

> Little voice from the corridor
> Floating the stairway up to her;

> Coming in laughter or in tears
> The little babble of scarce two years.
>
> Little form down the gravelled way
> Redcoated form in the cloudy day
> Bright little eyes of the flashing brown
> Do but look up, for *she's* looking down.
>
> How shall she bear it? the pain gone past
> Turned to a heartache indeed at last;
> Bonnie wee man in the coat of red
> She's sick with longing for you instead . . .

The final stanza of 'Exiled' speaks of the 'laughter that hangs on the edge of tears', a sentiment that seems to encapsulate the emotional fragility of that time.

By May of 1913, the small family of three was staying in Kensington, the London borough that was to be their home in later years. But on this first visit, no such certainties were in the air and Mary was still writing of Mabel's changing moods, as in the first part of the sonnet, 'The Face Withdrawn', dated 30 May:

> Clad in the dusks of twilight and the dawn;
> The shades of autumn and the lights of Spring
> Move o'er the face of which I brooding sing;
> The spirit thwarted tragically forlorn
> With many a grace half negligently worn;
> So strong, so weak! Oh such a mystic thing
> With meanings lucent, and bewildering
> So sweet in nearness, so divine withdrawn.

The two activists from Melbourne's women's suffrage movement were in London when Emily Wilding Davison, a member of the militant Women's Social and Political Union, ran onto the track at the Derby waving the WSPU's purple, white and green flag and grabbed the reins of King George V's horse. She died four days later from injuries sustained when she fell under the horse's hooves. Her funeral procession on 14 June brought parts of London to a standstill as some 6000 suffragettes (and some members of Men's Leagues for Women's Suffrage) marched silently behind suffrage banners through streets lined with thousands upon thousands of spectators. The procession wound from Victoria

Station to St George's Church in Bloomsbury and then to King's Cross Station, where the coffin was taken by train to Morpeth in the North of England for burial.[2] Mary and Mabel marched with the group representing the Irish Catholic Suffrage Society and Mary recounted later in *Woman Voter* that 'along the route was the populace, thoughtful, arrested. Its deep, solemn attentiveness to our marching thousands touched our eyes with the light of days to be'.[3] Speaking of the English suffrage movement, she declared to the members of the WPA: 'These women are breaking their bodies for the soul of England'.[4]

Mary and Mabel's stay in London stopped soon after this event and in July they boarded the *Malwa*, heading back for Melbourne. A letter written to Mary by Alice Grant Rosman, an Australian writer colleague who had been trying to set up a meeting between them in London, suggests that this departure may have been made in haste. Rosman wrote on 7 August that she had been looking forward to seeing Mary again, and 'quite apart from that it seems too bad that your stay should have been cut short in that way'.[5] Precisely why Mary, Mabel and Denis 'cut short' their trip and left England to return to Australia in July 1913 is not known, but it almost certainly was not Mary Fullerton's decision. Rosman had earlier written to Mary at the end of June, urging her to 'firmly refuse to be dragged back to Australia under any circumstances'.[6]

Mary wrote a long and complex poem (in pencil on P&O line paper) as they sailed into the 'Great Australian Bite [sic]' on 14 August. Called 'Miniatures', its opening lines speak of the poet's sorrow that the sea journey (and, presumably, the shared life they had enjoyed in England) was about to end:

> After weeks on land and sea
> (More I wish but never fewer)
> You are parting from me now . . .

In 'Miniatures', Mabel and Denis ('the winsome boy') are imaged as cameo portraits created by Nature. The poem recalls the woman 'of heroic mould' of the earlier poem, 'Won?', written a few months before Denis's birth. According to the poet, it was the 'mixed elements' given Mabel by Nature that caused her to become embroiled in the masquerade that was her marriage. Now it is suggested that the child, who is also from that mould, is part of destiny's plan to bring out the 'woman soul' of Mabel Singleton. Rather than 'Circumstance', the poet says, it is 'Destiny' that is 'Nature's mate/When she forms such miniatures'. The poem concludes with optimistic confidence:

> I perceive the full success
> Sometimes helper always viewer
> For with *Love* allied to *Will*
> (Goodness is a potent wooer)
> He will grow into his orb
> Mother by the power of yours
> Destiny is Nature's mate
> When she forms such miniatures.

A poem dated 28 November 1913, titled 'From the Heart' and one of the most intense Mary Fullerton ever wrote, gives some clues as to the possible circumstances surrounding the travellers' unscheduled return to Melbourne. This poem also casts light on why it was so crucial that Mary allowed herself to be 'dragged back to Australia'. Perhaps she even insisted on accompanying Mabel and her 'winsome boy'. Extending over several pages, it begins with the uncompromising line, 'Think I shall let you go'. The poet goes on to accuse her lover of being 'obstinate, weak, and proud', a 'butterfly on the wheel'. Referring back to 'Miniatures' where Mary had said Nature had created Mabel from 'mixed elements', she now reminds her:

> I shall not let you go
> Or give you up to a lie.
> You have some work to do
> You have a darling boy
> Your metal shall not be spoiled
> Because of the base alloy.

Later she pleads:

> The Past shall be dead
> When the Past is resigned;
> But still in your present
> Your Past is entwined.

> Foolish, defiant, and weak
> Knowing some day you *must*,
> Come to me, come to me dear
> Give me your trust.

The poem gives the impression that Mary Fullerton is engaged in a struggle with another for her lover, with someone from the past who will destroy her plan, the destiny she has envisaged for herself, Mabel and the 'darling boy'.

Hastily scrawled in pencil with no dedication, 'From the Heart' may have been written as an outlet for Mary's emotions and never intended for Mabel's eyes. The poet wrote one of her more formal, occasional sonnets to mark the end of 1913 and the beginning of the New Year. '1913–4', neatly written in ink and signed 'M.E.F.', expresses the poet's longings and her anticipation of further emotional turmoil with more restraint as it reaffirms her love for her friend. I have no doubt Mabel Singleton received this one:

> Old year go down in your vicissitudes;
> I care not, so you leave me still my friend
> Firmrooted through your long four seasons end.
> Though a New Year with things unknown intrudes
> New joys, new cares, new restless interludes
> Fresh hopes to lure, and broken tasks to mend;
> Old dreams to chase, new thoughts to comprehend
> That fling me through the gamuts of all moods.
>
> I care not what it bring of strife or change,
> The Year tiptoeing o'er the rosy hill
> Writ are its Days in sheath unknown and strange,
> If in each day your love is with me still;
> As in the days all fresh with morning dew,
> Nestles in each *my* Rose of Love for *You*.

What the new year of 1914 brought, less than three months after Mary wrote the fierce 'From the Heart', was the death on 22 February of Robert Singleton, Mabel's 73-year-old estranged husband. The cause of death given was heart failure. Perhaps it was her husband's failing health that precipitated Mabel's decision to return so suddenly to Australia in July 1913. It is possible she was even planning to return to him in order to achieve a reconciliation and to persuade him to change the terms of his will. Mary suggests in 'From the Heart' that her friend's 'Woman Soul' had partly awakened, then she had 'turned and dozed again/ When money gilded your yoke':

> So much has come to you
> Experience of Pain
> And quintessential Joy
> – And you have slept again!

As we know, Robert Singleton's will was not altered and Mabel was virtually disinherited. She was able to buy a house in Anderson Street, South Yarra, an inner Melbourne suburb, where she and Denis lived for several years; Denis thinks she may have borrowed on the money left for his education to purchase it. It appears that at some time during those years she was also a foster mother for her nephew Fred Singleton, the son of Robert Singleton's brother, one of two children who were born from his relationship with a Japanese woman. Fred was much older than Denis who thinks his cousin might have been at university when he and his mother left for England in 1921. Fred Singleton became a geologist and many years later, in 1938, he and his wife, Colwyn, stayed with Mabel and Mary in London when he attended a congress of scientists at Cambridge. Both Mabel and Mary seem to have enjoyed a close relationship with Fred and he sent them money every Christmas for a dinner and theatre outing when they lived in London. On one occasion Mary wrote a sonnet for him as thanks for a Christmas gift of a volume of Christina Rossetti's poems.

Mary reflects the racist views held in the newly-formed nation of Australia when she casually refers to Fred in a letter to Miles Franklin as 'Mabel's nephew the semi-Japanese'.[7] (Miles herself held virulent anti-Asian views). Bringing up a non-Caucasian youth must have been quite a challenge for Mabel Singleton in the early 1900s when even the Women's Political Association strongly endorsed the White Australia Policy. I would not be surprised, however, if her outlook was more liberal than that of writers such as Mary and Miles, committed as they were to the development of a nationalistic Australian literature in which being white and of British background was paramount.

Mabel Singleton eventually sold the house in South Yarra and moved to Ringwood near the foot of the Dandenongs. Now a heavily built-up outer suburb of Melbourne, Ringwood then was mainly bushland; Denis remembers riding his pony through the bush there. The woman who had been his nanny in South Yarra was a follower of the Italian educator, Maria Montessori, who had opened a school in Rome in 1907 where she developed an educational method that encouraged individual initiative and self-education on the part of the students. Denis's nanny, whom he describes as 'rather more than a nanny really', opened her own Montessori school at Ringwood and it is highly probable Mabel's decision to move there was at least partly so that Denis could attend this school. Her commitments with the Women's Political Association and the Women's Peace Army required her to work long hours, speaking constantly at meetings and rallies all over Melbourne, often late into the evening. A stable carer for Denis would have been of the utmost importance, and Mabel was also interested in progressive education.

Mary Fullerton continued to live with her mother and three unmarried sisters in Hawthorn after her return from England in 1913, working with Mabel in the WPA and sharing as much of her life as possible with her friend and her son. The poems to Mabel continued to spill from her pen throughout the years the two women were working side by side for the WPA and the Women's Peace Army. They range across many moods, often written in reaction to the changing moods of Mary's volatile friend. One undated poem is indeed called 'My Lady of Moods' and it is unusually abrupt and uncompromising:

> You say it now
> You would not say it then;
> Perverse: 'twill be the same
> Again, again.
>
> You said it then
> You will not say it now;
> Perverse: you'll be again
> I vow, I vow.

I say it now;
– The thought obtrudes –
It may be *two*
Can play at moods.

That you some day
May want the word;
It shall be deaf
My ear that heard.

It shall be cold
The cheek you touch;
Lady of Moods
You'll make me such.

But on the same page another poem appears, 'Ah Did You Wonder', in which the poet's angry mood has completely dissipated:

Ah' did you wonder
Wherefore I went and came?
So at the hov'ring moth
Wonders the flame.

Then no more wonder,
Oh sweet compelling soul;
Know that the needle must
Swing to the pole.

The poems Mary wrote during the years between 1914 and 1922 indicate that Mabel may have remained undecided for several years after her husband's death as to whether her 'destiny' lay with her friend. It seems too that Mary was committed to staying with her mother, whose health was becoming increasingly frail. And it becomes clear in later letters between Mabel Singleton and Miles Franklin that Mary's sisters, Emily, Sophie and Bell, did not altogether approve of her friendship with 'Mrs Singleton'. Perhaps when Mabel and Denis made the move to England and Mary decided to follow (after her mother died), the distance between Australia and England made it possible for her to share her life completely with her friend at last. Living in cosmopolitan London, she was far from the gaze of her conservative Melbourne sisters.

'I TO THE GUARD BELONG'

'From the Heart', that long and passionate poem Mary Fuller-ton wrote at the end of 1913, contained some strange notions I struggled to understand. These lines, for instance:

> Trust me who feels the truth,
> Even hard difficult truth
> Since the first day we met
> With love and with ruth,
> I who have touched the heart
> Of the world's old wrong
> (Meekly I say it here)
> I to the *guard* belong

What was this 'guard' that was so important it was underlined? The poet also says a little later that she is on the '"shining side" . . . With those who unfaltering walk/The upward track'. The poem concludes with an exhortation to her beloved friend, Mabel Singleton, to recognise her 'Soul'. This mysterious 'Woman Soul' Mary writes about so often is connected with her knowledge of the truth because she belongs to the 'guard':

> I too oh love, my love
> Who make deeper appeal
> Because past all I *know*
> Is all I *feel*
> No one knows you so well
> – The flash was mine
> That knew the splendid Soul
> And knew it thine.
> . . .
> You know I shall never let
> The wilful hand of you free
> You know the *accomplice Boy*
> Is accomplice unto *me*.
> Come – leave all the arguments –
> All of our strivings leave;
> Face to the final pole

Under the flag "achieve",
No more uncertain dear,
Of aim, object or place
Follow the destined road
Come and live out your face.

It seems that the 'accomplice Boy', Mabel's little son (the 'winsome boy' of 'Miniatures') is also implicated. He is Mary's accomplice in this endeavour, not his mother's. And Mabel's beauty – her 'face' that Mary eulogised in so many poems – appears to hold the key to her destiny. I needed to explore more of Mary Fullerton's work and to turn again to ideas that were 'in the air' at the time this poem was written.

Mary wrote a series of six unpublished sonnets called 'A Photograph' during the time she spent at Mabel's family home at Walsall in the beginning of 1913. The poems refer to a photographic portrait of the young Mabel Jupp that hung on the drawing-room wall there (which may well be the portrait Denis Singleton showed me when I visited him in London). In the first sonnet, Mary links the look in the eyes of the young woman with the portrait of Mary Wollstonecraft in the National Portrait Gallery: 'it blent / Something of all the woe of every heart'. It is the look of the woman soul:

'Tis not a portrait in a measured frame,
A picture of a girl of midland town;
It bears beneath it every woman's name,
Of every time as though 'twere written down;
– The old-time woman's soul, the soul to be
A recapitulation and a prophecy.

The third sonnet forecasts that Mabel Singleton will become 'A living woman symbol of the race, / Whose soul of beauty streams from beauteous face'. Sonnet Five analyses the poet's own debt to Mary Wollstonecraft:

I have an old time portrait, calm and cool
Yet in my school-girl eye a glow methinks;
As one who knows it is her wine she drinks
Wise with a knowledge learned not in a school . . .

The final sonnet of this series reiterates Mary's belief in the destiny of her friend and also elucidates her own role in the process:

> Breast on dear woman, face the hill,
> The destined must be done though it may wait
> A season while we fumble at the gate;
> Your work is waiting and you must fulfill.
> About that pictured mouth is mighty will
> And though its pain be much, its power is great,
> Your soul is made to rule and dominate
> Your face is made to lift, inspire and thrill.
>
> Dear, I was first made conscious and alive,
> But *you* were given a dower that is not mine;
> That makes your pathway easy where I strive,
> You know what I would say – that CHARM is thine
> A power more great than learning, instinct, pelf
> – Transform that pictured face, fulfill yourself.

In this series of sonnets, the relationship between the poet and her friend is similar to that in the later poem, 'From the Heart'. It appears the poet possesses a special consciousness that enables her to recognise the potential in the woman she loves. Mary reiterates this theme in many of the personal poems she wrote in the early part of the twentieth century. The answer to the problem of how to make sense of these unfamiliar ideas may lie among the sexological theories that were being developed around the turn of the century, even though Mary herself resisted the discourse of abnormality that was promoted in the work of Havelock Ellis, whose *Studies in the Psychology of Sex* first appeared in 1897.

Evolutionary theory was an important influence on all scientific thought in the era I examined. We live now in a post-Freudian age. Our culture is saturated with Freudian assumptions and terms, such as the unconscious, that do not depend on our actually reading his work, or even on our agreement or disagreement with his theoretical position. Charles Darwin's work influenced the generations that succeeded him in the latter half of the nineteenth century in a similar way. Mary Fullerton was born into a post-Darwinian world, but she was sufficiently close to its beginnings (*The Origin of Species* was published in 1859 and she was born in 1868 to grow up aware of evolutionary theory and to be contemporary with the social movements and "scientific" developments such as Social Darwinism, eugenics and sexological theory that grew out of its influence.

Mary talked in 'Memoirs' about being 'an unobtrusive but noting listener' of adult conversations when a child in Gippsland. These conversations were her introduction to what she called 'undigested Darwinism . . . Literals such as the creation of Adam and Eve had to go'.[1] Evolutionary theory had revolutionised previous understandings of the natural order. In contradiction to the Christian account of divine creation, it proposed a continuum between animals and mankind and described a continuing process in which species change, develop and become extinct. But Darwin wrote of the 'descent' as well as the 'ascent' of mankind, and indicated that the future of the race depended on, among other things, the sexual health of its members.

Whereas previous distinctions between reproductive and non-reproductive sex had emphasised the act itself, in sexological theory a new conceptual alignment emerged between sexuality that was normal and natural, on the one hand, and deviant sexuality on the other. This distinction was located in individual types of people rather than simply in sexual or, in the terms of religious discourse, sinful acts. The homosexual became a species, and so did the heterosexual. The odds would seem to be stacked against someone like Mary Fullerton, whose primary relationship was with another woman, being able to consider herself anything but unnatural or abnormal. She managed to circumvent positioning herself that way, however, because she did not consider herself homosexual but asexual.

Mary's asexual "sexual" identity is one that may have been taken up by many spinsters in the early part of the twentieth century, particularly by those involved in the suffrage and allied political movements. These were women who performed, through their activism, a kind of "social motherhood" in which their family was the society they lived in. It was an identity that, paradoxically, could accommodate (at least privately) conscious same-sex desire and perhaps even what we would understand as lesbian sexual practices. And rather than Havelock Ellis's theory of congenital sexual inversion which is the most commonly known sexological theory today, the ideas that may have appealed to such women belonged to one of his colleagues, the English utopian socialist, writer, and sexologist, Edward Carpenter.

Carpenter gathered around him a formidable circle of friends from among the intellectuals of England. Although he wrote prolifically, his writing was less easily classifiable than that of his more "scientific" colleagues like Ellis, and his reputation during his lifetime was based partly on his charismatic personality. One of his friends, the novelist E. M. Forster, described him in a radio address in 1944 as someone who had been 'a poet, prose writer, a prophet, a socialist, a mystic, a manual labourer, an anti-vivisectionist, an art-critic, etcetera'.[2] What Forster, himself a closeted homosexual, declined to mention in this list were Carpenter's radical views on 'homogenic' or 'Uranian' love experienced by what he dubbed 'the intermediate sex'. This category, to which Carpenter felt he belonged, comprised individuals he perceived as standing midway between the two poles of humanity – male and female. Although his emphasis was on male Uranians, or Urnings as they were sometimes termed, Carpenter wrote quite extensively on female members of the intermediate sex too, proclaiming them to be 'often fitted for remarkable work . . . even as a ruler of a country'. The love of such women he described as 'a powerful passion, almost of heroic type, and capable of inspiring to great deeds'.[3]

Carpenter's writings had already found an audience in the colonies before the end of the nineteenth century. Frank Bongiorno quotes the emigrant English socialist, H. H. Champion, writing to Carpenter from Australia in 1895: '[a] good many here read & appreciate Towards Democracy. There are more to be had here & if you care to send a few – & your sex pamphlet & any others I can sell them through the paper'.[4] Henry Hyde Champion was Vida Goldstein's brother-in-law, so Carpenter's writings were definitely circulating among the feminist socialists of Melbourne, of whom Mary Fullerton was one. Mary herself spoke publicly on Edward Carpenter in a lecture she gave to the women of the Victorian Socialist Party in May 1919. The *Socialist* reported the event and said 'a good muster of women' attended the 'Pleasant Wednesday Afternoon', but did not indicate the content of the address. It is safe to say that it is more likely to have been about his political writings than his work on sexuality.[5] Whatever the subject, the reference proves that Mary was familiar with Carpenter's writings and interested enough in them to make him the subject of a lecture.

It is not difficult to understand why Edward Carpenter would appeal to Mary Fullerton. Like her, he was concerned with 'the questions of the heart and soul' in his work. Like hers, his personal life and writing were part of a wider vision of how the world might be. Noel Greig describes Carpenter as wishing 'to link all aspects of himself – the inner and the outer, the intellectual and the spiritual, the physical and the emotional – with all aspects of the world'.[6]

Carpenter's book-length philosophical poem, *Towards Democracy*, the first part of which was published in the 1880s, may have provided Mary with another version of friendship to adapt to suit her emotional and political needs. Like the earlier Emerson, Carpenter placed friendship at the highest level of human relations. *Towards Democracy* is a utopian vision of a new classless world order in which politics is based on the common bond of friendship rather than the profit-driven, economic motives of capitalism. Furthermore, and here he differs from the transcendental Emerson, Carpenter associates friendship with the body, with love and passion, between men and women *and* between members of the same sex. He describes 'the love of women for each other' as 'so rapt, intense, so confiding-close, so burning-passionate/To unheard deeds of sacrifice, of daring and devotion, prompting'.[7]

Mary Fullerton wrote a long unpublished poem called 'The Immemorial Woman Slave' that is reminiscent of Carpenter's *Towards Democracy* in style and content. The narrators in both have a kind of 'cosmic consciousness' similar to the quality Mary perceived in her own portrait in the series, 'A Photograph'. Mary herself later used this term when she recounted to Miles Franklin an experience that inspired a poem called 'The Charwoman': 'I *was* that woman whom I saw one night going up the stairs to our political club in Melb. It was a queer moment when she and I looked into each other's eyes as she stood aside to let me pass'. She interprets the moment as one of 'cosmic consciousness', something that is experienced occasionally by those on a higher evolutionary level.[8]

The emphasis in Mary's epic vision of the future, unlike Carpenter's, is on the central role of women in the transformation of society. The poem gives some clues as to what is meant by the 'Woman Soul' and why Mary Fullerton perceived this figure to be so important, not only to her friend but also to the whole future of society. It urges middle-class, politically-conscious women to rescue their working-class sisters from their position of slavery so that they may have a chance to develop their 'woman souls'. Though undated, the poem's suffragist content suggests it belongs to the period of Mary's involvement with the Women's Political Association. 'The Immemorial Woman Slave' bears strong links with 'From the Heart', expounding a similar theme on a more cosmic level.

In his book, *The Intermediate Sex*, written several years after *Towards Democracy*, Carpenter identifies lovers of their own sex as 'Uranians', whose important function is to act as 'advanced souls', to form the 'advance guard' for his vision of an egalitarian, compassionate society. 'Uranian people', he writes, 'may be destined to form the advance guard of that great movement which will one day transform the common life by substituting the bond of personal affection and compassion for the monetary, legal and other external ties which now control and confine society'.[9] It seems evident that Mary Fullerton had read *The Intermediate Sex*, published in 1908, by the time she wrote 'From the Heart' in 1913. Describing herself in this poem as a member of the 'guard', she also says she belongs 'With those who unfaltering walk / The upward track'. The upward track is that of evolution, along which the 'advanced souls' march.

Many women were inspired to write to Edward Carpenter after reading his writing on what he called the 'intermediate sex'. Today, the term is commonly understood to denote a person who feels they are trapped in the body of the opposite sex, but that meaning derives from the earlier writing of Karl Ulrichs in the 1860s. Ulrichs' writing on Urnings was Carpenter's inspiration for his Uranians (from *Uranos*, Greek for heaven; 'urning' is the German version), but he transformed Ulrichs' conception into a positive, even desirable attribute. The archives at the Sheffield Library in the north of England (where the Cambridge-educated Carpenter settled with his working-class lover, George Merrill) contain letters by women written between 1913 and 1925.[10]

One from an English-born Brisbane woman in 1914 is typical of the sentiments the women express. 'I belong to this class myself', she wrote: 'I have always been much attached to my own sex, and though by no means a man-hater, have always preferred women as companions and friends . . . Since reading your book it has been a tremendous relief to find there are so many others in the same position, and more especially that you think it is a sign of evolution towards higher things'.[11] Another woman, known as KO, who contributed to a debate about spinsters in the English feminist magazine, *The Freewoman*, arguing for chastity, also wrote personally to Carpenter three years later in 1915 after having read *The Intermediate Sex*. In her letter she said she believed she belonged 'to that class' and asked him if there was any way she could get in touch with others 'of the same temperament'.[12]

In this period, before it became co-opted into the medical discourse of abnormality and disease, being Uranian could also imply greatness. I came across this extract from the 1914 diary of a young Englishwoman in Tierl Thompson's book, *Dear Girl*, in which she talks about discussing the 'intermediate sex' with her close woman friend: 'A quiet evening – Ruth read aloud a little from Edward Carpenter – his poem on the Urnings led us to talk of the 'intermediate sex'; we wondered whether the great teachers Christ and Buddha belonged to this category, having in themselves the experiences and nature of either sex – then we talked of the procreation of children by the intermediate sex, either naturally or by thought and ended in a confusion of ideas, having lost the thread of our discussion.[13]

Carpenter's writings on the intermediate sex provided some

kind of avenue for women who loved women to view themselves in a positive light, but they were also problematic for them to adapt. Respectable women did not talk of their sexual desires except in terms of the desire for marriage and motherhood. Even most feminist advocates of women's capacity for sexual desire still incorporated it into the belief that ultimate fulfilment for women lay in motherhood. And men like Carpenter, who considered themselves to be in sympathy with feminist ideals, found it difficult to reconcile women and homosexuality.

Carpenter's problems in writing about 'homogenic' women rested on two important issues. First, according to the prevailing thinking of the time, for women to be sexual with each other they would need an active or, in other words, masculine temperament (as was the case in theories of sexual inversion). Men's sexual nature was thought to be already active, whether it be homosexual or heterosexual. Secondly, and most crucially, if increasing numbers of middle-class and educated women joined the feminist movement and eschewed marriage, it was believed that the 'sex instinct' might increasingly disappear in such women and add to the threat of the degeneracy of the race. This is the underside to Carpenter's 'advanced soul' theory as it applied to women.

If homogenic women could only be actively sexual if they were 'mannish' in temperament and since this was a term of abuse used against suffragists in general, it was understandable that it was an epithet they were anxious to avoid. But within the terms of Carpenter's theories on 'advanced souls', homogenic women could be beyond the 'sex instinct', they could be leaders, but they could not be sexual beings without the risk of losing their status as 'womanly' women. This was a conundrum that Mary Fullerton seems to have been unable to resolve completely in spite of her passion for Mabel Singleton.

Even if she could not construct her love for her friend as sexual, Mary did manage to fit Mabel and her son into her vision for a future that shares similarities with Carpenter's homogenic ideas. Mabel Singleton appears to have been a wonderful example of what Edward Carpenter regarded as the 'normal and perfect' homogenic, or Uranian woman. His description of such a woman in *The Intermediate Sex* is uncannily apt. Described as 'a type in which the body is thoroughly feminine and gracious', her 'inner nature', by contrast, 'is to a great extent masculine, a temperament active, brave, originative, somewhat decisive, not too emotional; fond of outdoor-life, of games and sports, of science, politics, or even business; good at organisation, and well-pleased with positions of responsibility'.[14]

As well as meeting the criteria laid down by Carpenter for the 'perfect' homogenic woman, Mabel also fulfilled his ideal of the mother of the future. All her life she was concerned with physical health and natural foods, eventually becoming a vegetarian. During the 1910s she undertook a course to become a physical culture teacher, a profession that she was unable to take up because of an accident she suffered (she was struck by a car as she stepped off a tram in Melbourne). Mabel's interest in the 'Dalcroze' system of musical education devised in the early 1900s by Swiss music teacher and composer, Emile Jaques-Dalcroze, and in Maria Montessori's progressive ideas on education, also made her eminently suitable.

Mary Fullerton understood her role in the upbringing of her friend's son to be crucial. Her belief that her destiny was complementary to Mabel's seems to have depended upon the construction of herself as beyond personal motherhood. Her role as guide in the awakening of Mabel's soul, a process in which the 'accomplice Boy' was her ally, made the two women, in a sense, complementary "mothers". Mary's love was the guiding force in this process, this 'mating'. As a result, the quality of the women's friendship transcended the ordinary connotations of the term, elevating it to a kind of "marriage".

Mary eventually wrote a poem that celebrated her friend's achievement of her destiny as an 'accomplished soul'. Apparently written for Mabel's birthday in 1916, it is called simply '40' and signed 'With more love than can be spoken or written, M'. It seems that the poet believed her lover had indeed begun to throw off the 'hereditary dole' she referred to in the sonnet series, 'A Photograph', in order to become that 'living woman symbol of the race':

> Now you begin to live
> For life has most to give
> When the first youth's gone
> And the vacillations of the soul are done.

The poem concludes:

> Forty – alive – complete
> *Aware* on your own firm feet
> Oh love awake and whole
> I greet an accomplished soul.
>
> I greet you and your years
> Almost I wean, with tears
> Wholly with joy, all without fears
> See you near not afar
> Achieved, not *To Be*
> At last, ah at last
> You *Are*.

The writing that most clearly shows Mary Fullerton's debt to Edward Carpenter is contained in the curious novella-length story she submitted to a publisher's competition in London in 1922, not long after she left Australia to rejoin Mabel. *Clare* (the piece that is partly autobiographical, at least as far as the narrator's childhood is concerned) shared the prize with another story and they were published together, anonymously, under the title, *Two Women: Clare, Margaret*, in 1923. The competition was for a book of 'self-revelation', described in somewhat tautological terms by the publishers as 'the best true autobiographical Life-Story'. Mary was careful to distance herself from the narrator of *Clare* when writing to her family about it: 'Knowing that there would be seasoned writers in the field I determined to invent a character that had not been done ever before. I took the type of woman who has no sex side to her, and put her in circumstances where she practically is compelled by Fate to marry. The reverse of everything usual you see'.[15]

If we compare the narrator of the novel, Clare Langton, and the poet of the love poems to Mabel Singleton, we can see, however, just how much Mary's own feelings were involved in the 'type' she explored. Clare Langton's mentor, who is also the father of the young woman to whom she is passionately attached, gives her the nickname, Urania, to be used 'for private pleasure' and chosen, he says, on the basis of his insight into her character and nature. 'Your type is not readily understood', he warns, and offers to lend her a book 'that will give you a clue to the application'.[16] In a later conversation, Clare confirms that after reading the book she feels the name Urania 'fits', although she is worried that it is 'too splendid' for her. In exchange, she lends her benefactor Emerson's essay, 'Friendship'. It is more than likely, I believe, that the book in which Clare learns about Uranians was one of Edward Carpenter's.

In some ways *Clare* reads like a rather desperate attempt to hold on to a way of thinking that was rapidly becoming outdated by the time it was written in the early 1920s, bearing in mind that it may have been based on an earlier manuscript. The post-war climate was quite different from the time when Mary Fullerton had fashioned her poet/lover persona in her poems to Mabel Singleton, during the years in which they were active suffragists in the WPA in Melbourne. Spinsterhood and celibacy, important elements of Mary's self-construction, had come under increasing attack and no longer held the currency they had acquired in the late nineteenth century as components of a particular feminist political strategy.

A strand of feminism that concentrated on women's equality in marriage and extolled motherhood had become the dominant form by the 1920s. The writing of doctor and sex reformer, Marie Stopes, is an example of this "domestic" feminism. As an ambiguous overlap grew between spinsterhood, homosexuality and frigidity, there was a tendency, developed through the popularisation of sexology and psychology, to regard close female friendships with suspicion . Freud's relocation of the sex instinct from biology to the psyche and its reconfiguration as "drive" was also a threat; his notion of sublimation was a far cry from the transmutation of the physical to the spiritual favoured by many suffragists. By 1933, the situation had become so confusing that Mary wrote wryly to Miles Franklin: 'I fear me half the world is tangled morally. Lord, is it a whirl of dominating chromosomes held in through the Puritan era? The turn of the wheel. Expect Miles any day to hear that MEF is a pervert invert or any other vert even convert to "ways that are dark". I'll send a cable when I feel the repressions bursting the lid off the volcano – the real I *am* according to Freud Esq'.[17]

But even in 1923, the tone of 'Clare' is earnest and often defiantly defensive of its narrator's position as beyond the sex instinct; it also engages indirectly with notions of frigidity and lesbianism. On one occasion, a friend says to Clare: 'You and your kind are a protest against the oversexualisation of civilisation. If you're unnatural, it's because it is unnatural'. Clare replies: 'It may indeed be so. At any rate, my kind exists. I'm not such an uncompanioned freak as some would think'.[18]

Edward Carpenter's Uranian theory was always a marginal theory of homosexuality, especially in its positive depiction of the Uranian as above the societal norm. By the time *Clare* was written, Uranianism had largely been incorporated into the medical theories of sexual inversion. Dr Marie Stopes replied to a woman who asked her to write a book on the subject of lesbianism: 'I should be very pleased to write a book on what – don't be hurt – I consider the disease of uranianism. So any information would be recorded with that in view. You may find in me a doctor – a saviour – but *not* a champion'.[19]

Rather than seeing Mary Fullerton's *Clare* as a celebration of the 'advanced soul', the publishers seem to have chosen the prize-winners because they depicted contrasting extreme 'types' of women. The Publishers Note that prefaces *Two Women* defined these types as 'the subnormal and the supernormal woman'. The highly-sexed protagonist of *Margaret* corresponds to the first category, while the narrator of *Clare*, who claims to be beyond the sex instinct, comes under the second. 'Mr Havelock Ellis' provided a quote for the advertisement of *Two Women* in the press, locating the stories within a medical and sexological, as well as a literary framework: 'Not only well written as stories, but they should prove helpful in making clear to their readers some real and difficult problem [sic] of modern life'.[20] Mrs C.A. Dawson Scott, who reviewed *Two Women* for the English literary magazine, *The Bookman*, was unable to find a central narrative in *Clare*: 'The first [story] is entirely genuine, but as the woman does not wish to love, marry or bear children, it lacks human interest. It is in fact like beads in a box, beads that have not been strung on a cord'.[21]

ENGLAND: NEW BEGINNINGS

Denis Singleton remembers waving goodbye to the little girl next door from the footplate of the train as he and his mother left Ringwood for the docks when he was ten years old. But he does not know exactly why Mabel Singleton took him to England to live in 1921. She may have returned to her homeland for Denis's education as he suggests; the other reasons he offers – her 'disappointments' in Melbourne concerning her marriage and the accident that left her unable to teach physical training – may also have played a part. Mabel's brother, Dr Ralph Jupp, who had been so solicitous during the 1912 visit home, died four days before they arrived in London on this second journey, but Denis believes this tragedy was unexpected and not the reason for their return.

The death of her brother was not the only loss Mabel experienced on her homecoming. A few months later on 28 January 1922, the very day Mary Fullerton sailed from Melbourne to rejoin her friend, Mabel's father died suddenly. She was at Walsall, because her stepmother was unwell, when her father 'took ill shivering during the night and died quietly . . . gone within an hour'.[1] Mabel felt the loss keenly, telling Mary's sisters in a letter that 'now that father and Ralph have died, Denis and I are the only two left of our family'. She felt an affection for her stepmother but 'only because of her goodness to father and not because we have anything in common'.[2]

Mary's arrival in England, just a few weeks after this second death in the space of a few months, was not the celebration Mabel had planned. She had cabled Fred Singleton about her father's death on the day Mary embarked on her voyage, but it had been too late to convey the news to her. Mary eventually received it in a letter Mabel sent to Port Said, so she was not entirely unprepared.

But by the time she reached her destination after weeks at

sea, her friend and Denis were both suffering from whooping-cough and Mabel had to insist to her doctor that she 'must' go to meet the ship when it docked at Tilbury.[3] Mary was unwell too, still recovering from her mother's death the previous June and from the influenza that had threatened her own life. Thus the beginning of their new life together encompassed illness, sadness and loss, but it was also the first time the two women had set up house together. This they did in Letchworth in Hertfordshire, about twenty miles along the train line from central London.

Late in 1922, after renting in Letchworth for several months, Mabel bought Fairhaven, a charming house with a large garden that brought pleasure to all three of its inhabitants. Apart from a prolific flower garden, there were fruit trees and vegetables; Mary and Mabel enjoyed their own currants and fresh greens and also made gooseberry jelly and plum jam. Denis made a pond from clay and cement and filled it with newts when he was home from the local private school he attended. (When Mary was recounting this to her sisters, she said she had suggested putting in 'some leeches too a la Jeeraling Creek', referring to a childhood haunt in Gippsland). Denis's school, St Christophers, was a co-educational school, set up by a Miss King with whom Mabel became friendly. Co-education was considered quite progressive in the 1920s; perhaps surprisingly, it had been favoured by many suffragists. Vida Goldstein and her sisters had opened a co-educational preparatory school in Melbourne in the 1890s, believing 'this promoted a more rational relationship between the sexes'.[4]

The official story concerning Mary's move to England was that she had come to act as Mabel's companion and in order to further her own writing. Though true, this account glosses over the strength of the two women's commitment to each other. We know of Mary's deep involvement in her relationship with her friend from the poems she wrote; Mabel's feelings about Mary remain for the most part tantalisingly out of reach since she was not a poet and no letters survive between the two, although a trace of their correspondence appears in the typed and handwritten sheets of Mary's poems. Sometimes Mary would answer a line from a letter with a poem, as in the undated sonnet called 'An Answer', which is headed with the words '"Sometimes I think you are like a child" – Letter from MS to MF'. On another occasion, Mary wrote a poem called 'Dual Natures', which begins, 'Am I a contradiction?' in answer to the line from a letter from Mabel: 'What a strange woman you are, in some ways how contradictory'.

We can glean some sense of Mabel's feelings about her friend's move to England to join her from a letter she wrote to the Fullerton sisters (in Melbourne) soon after Mary arrived. After alluding to Mary's poor state of health – 'When I first saw her she looked very much better than when we left Melbourne, a little fatter,' – Mabel approaches the subject of Mary's life with her: 'It is difficult to say just what I want to about having her with us. I must take a woman companion and *infinitely* prefer someone like Mary who has her own work and yet who is at the same time all I need in the other way'. Just what 'the other way' refers to is not clear – close friend, carer for Denis, perhaps? – but what does become clear is that Mary had very little money and that her friend was at least partly supporting her. Mabel then drops her formal tone as she explains: 'As to the money part, I haven't much patience to talk about it, I never have, and *never shall* value money except for its use, and I ask no better use to put what little happens to be mine than to share it with Mary and Denis, the two people I want to have with me as much as possible'. Further on she confesses, 'Mary is far more to me than all my relations put together. Perhaps the theosophists are right, that we live again and again and Mary and I were friends before; except that she is a few stages ahead of me in her development'.[5] Echoes from a different perspective of the evolutionary 'upward track'?

Mabel's not altogether successful attempt to position Mary Fullerton as simply a congenial woman companion indicates that she felt some explanation was needed on her part for the fact that Mary had left Australia. It is apparent from the careful way she starts her letter that the family did not endorse Mary's move to join her friend and, at least to some extent, held 'Mrs Singleton' responsible.

It seems from the tone of a letter Mary wrote two years later to tell her sisters of a visit to Fairhaven by their English vicar cousin, Hugh Fullerton, that she too was eager for her sisters to approve of her new "family" and of their life together: 'He arrived at about half past 11am. Mabel had a slap-up dinner for him – not quite on arrival of course. We had our own green peas, boiled fresh salmon and accessories and some nice pudding stuff in variety, finished up with fruit and nuts and bread and cheese then coffee and he had his pipe. Not that Hugh is a big eater but M had things nice in honor of this visit and treated him well in every way. He stayed till a five forty pm train . . . Hugh does not seem a bit old-ish although sixty-six-past. He is young in face and habits. A fine tall man well-made and not parsonical in manner at all . . . He told me he thought Mabel a fine woman and a fine looking one too. Denis was away at Wembley with the school . . . so Hugh did not see him but he saw his photo . . . Hugh was so pleased to see me here and loved the place, thinks Fairhaven no end nice and so it is. "I felt I wanted to see you in your environment", he said. So I told him I suppose it was to see if Mabel looked a decent and fit companion for me. He retorted that he thought I might be *making her up*'. [6]

Many years later, after Mary's death, Mabel was to write openly to Miles Franklin about how those sisters in Melbourne had inter-preted her part in Mary's move to England to live with her. On one occasion, she wrote of Emily Fullerton, who by then lived in Sydney and whom Miles knew very well: 'she has been more understanding about Mary's and my friendship and more appre-ciative of what I did for Mary, than any of the others. There has been a lot of bad feeling towards me . . . Yes! "Mary's soul was har-ried" beyond belief and *I had to get her away*'.[7] In a later letter she reiterated her sense of their disapproval, saying that two of the sisters 'thought badly of me for bringing Mary to England: how little they know or understand – I could not have kept her away, had I tried. She would not have lived long in Australia anyway'.[8]

I have found no information about the feelings of Mary's mar-ried sisters and brother towards Mabel, but Lyd Chester, the sister Mary was closest to as a child, did visit the two women in London. She was accompanied by her daughter, Sophie, who later settled in London and became closely involved with the Singleton/Fullerton menage. Lyd wrote to 'Soph, Pem and Belle' on their arrival in the June of 1925 that 'Mary is looking thin and frail same as she was, but is now going to have some treatment to see if she can get a bit more flesh on her bones. Mrs Singleton is well, works hard at her office, has been most kind to us since our arrival'.[9]

The small family of three spent several weeks in Scotland during the August summer holidays of 1922 and later that year Mabel bought the domestic hiring agency in Kensington that she was to run until 1948. Her commuting from Letchworth to London meant that Mary looked after many of Denis's daily needs. Mabel still took her responsibilities as a mother seriously, however, and performed the sort of juggling acts working mothers are very familiar with. When Denis left his overcoat in a cloakroom and his friend, Bobbie, lost his camera during a school excursion, Mary reported home: 'This morning Mabel had to readjust her day and go off to Wembley after the coat and possibly to hear of the camera if it was put in the lost parcels there'.[10]

As well as sharing the care of the young schoolboy, Mary wrote prolifically during this period, submitting articles and short stories to English and Australian newspapers. Although she had some success with publication, she was grateful when Emily sent her thirty pounds, explaining that 'the pay here for odd work is not what it is cracked up to be'.[11]

At fifty-four years old and with a history of poor health, Mary fell ill early in 1923 'with severe congestion all over me except for my lungs though I think that was what the doctors feared would develop'. She was attended by two women doctors and a trained nurse for over a month, creating a further drain on her limited resources. Yet she wrote to her sisters with characteristic self-effacement: 'It was worse on the whole for Mabel than for me she worried so much and it was an upset in every way'.[12] Being notified of her win in the London publishing firm's literary competition in March must have helped to lift Mary's spirits; so must the 125 pounds she received as her share of the prize money for *Clare*, even if she had to wait until November to get the cheque.

For Mabel's birthday in 1924, Mary wrote a sonnet that reaffirmed her love for her friend. It is the clearest proof that the move to England was not made primarily in order to further her writing career, but was a product of her long-held belief that their 'destinies' lay together. Writing at Ehrwald in Austria (where Mabel took part in the 'Breathing Culture' course that Celie John also attended) during a holiday with Mabel and Denis that took in several European countries, the poet revisits familiar themes:

> A world away from where I met you first,
> Now other wheels of stars above me shine,
> Far from the Southern Cross, pure, opaline
> The friends we met amongst are all dispersed,
> Another race I see around me nursed
> Time has been envious, with sure design
> Stealing the Past to leave my heart athirst
> For all the dear familiars that were mine.
>
> Yet all the thieves' most urgent pillaging
> Of things held dear – the distant things I knew,
> And all the threat'ning swoop of Condor wing,
> And all that Pirate Change can ever do,
> Will leave me rich, and glad, and conquering,
> As long as they that rob me leave me you.

This birthday sonnet is the last of the dated poems to Mabel that survive, except for a few written in the 1940s as Mary Fullerton reviewed her long life. It is possible no more were written. The two women's circumstances had changed; no longer did Mary need to pour her emotions onto paper as she had during the turbulent decade when she and Mabel were often parted and when, it seems, Mabel was undecided about their relationship. While this 1924 poem contains sadness at the loss of the poet's 'familiars' and her homeland, as well as apprehension at her own fragile health and impending old age, an overall feeling of calmness and deep joy pervades it.

The pleasant routine the two women established at Fairhaven was to last only a short time. At the end of 1924 Mabel sold the house and the three moved into another rented house nearby. Why this happened is not known, but Denis's explanation is a likely one: that his mother 'ran out of funds'. In March 1925 Mary wrote to her sisters that she had attended a 'discussion class' at Fairhaven where the new owner had given her 'some violets for Mrs Singleton from the group of them under the gorse there. I told you about them last year. The scent is filling the room as I write'.[13]

This matter-of-fact revelation struck me as quite poignant, especially with the extra resonance it contains when we consider the poetry Mary wrote to Mabel, in which violets are a recurring image of desire: 'purple violets of joy' with 'scents to soothe and thrill'. The 1925 violets were of the English variety, but the Austral violet had earlier acquired a particular metaphorical significance for this poet. It is reputed to have no scent and yet in Mary's poems it emits a powerful fragrance that seems to stand for unsanctioned desire, as in the opening of the first of two connected untitled sonnets that bear the handwritten dedication: "To You who thought of me in absence. M.E.F.":

> They say the Austral violet has no scent,
> That into colour all her beauty flows;
> Or to her heart the urgent sunlight goes,
> And quickly steals that gift munificent,
> So ere you gather her, her balm is spent:
> Then in what Sabbath dell shall I suppose
> You straying, found and loved and gathered those
> Above whose breath I but this moment bent?

It seems that the rented house in Letchworth was a temporary measure while Mabel waited to secure a flat in London. Another possibility for the sale of Fairhaven might be that commuting the twenty miles by train to the agency proved too much for her. In any event, by June 1925 she and Mary were living in a flat in West Kensington. Denis went to board at Frensham school near Farnham until he started an apprenticeship in 1928 at his cousin's electrical business in London, when he resumed living with his mother and her companion. 'A real man yet a lovable kid', Mary was to report to Miles Franklin about the 17-year-old Denis.[14]

Between 1925 and 1931, when they moved into 181c High Street, Mary and Mabel lived in a series of rented flats in the Kensington area. Mary described one as a 'nice little flat small but cosy. Again we have a large bedroom which Mabel and I share'.[15] Another was so small they found it more convenient to entertain friends for dinner at Mabel's office: 'we turn it on such occasions into a residence, and find it more roomy than this flat which is "two by three"'.[16] One flat they moved into at the end of 1928 'was considerably needing cleaning and fixing etc. Departing devils had grabbed all tearoffable fixtures and the electric light too . . . This is a nice flat and cheap, we got the chance and grabbed it quickly'.[17]

In her frequent 'home' letters to her sisters, Mary often gave thumbnail sketches of the everyday lives of the three, such as the last few lines of this one written in November 1929: 'It is now Monday night and I've been writing this in bed after having a read. Denis sitting sprawling in an easy chair by the fire reading *Tess*. Mabel breaking in a new secretary at the office'.[18] In a long letter describing their Christmas in 1929, she details the theatre party of Christmas eve which included Mabel's secretary, Jean Hamilton: 'the whole thing of course Fred [Singleton's] Xmas present . . . Then on Xmas morning we lay in for a rest till Denis awakening about nine came into our room with our Christmas presents quite in the old style'.[19]

Miles Franklin replied to the letter she received about that memorable Christmas: 'Mary me gurrl . . . I rejoiced in your Christmas. It sounded real good and the 32 packets in Mabel's pillow case, and your books, and to have such a lion as Jean H, and to go to Celie John's cottage. Whoopee!'.[20] (What *did* Mabel get in those packets?) Mary spoke more personally to Miles than to her sisters about her feelings for Denis, breaking off one letter saying: 'I must stop and help the boy, he looks so wistful now and then, I think realizes the plunge real going forth into the world; though very manly he is after all not yet twenty and has been so much with us especially with me that I don't like to imagine myself with him gone. Like my own son methinks'.[21]

In mid 1930, Mabel started looking for new premises for her office as the building at 158 High Street, Kensington, was to be demolished. By the end of the year, she had found the ideal location 'nearly opposite where she is now, a place that gives offices and living apartments under the same roof'.[22] This was at 181c High Street and the 'living apartment' was the large top-floor flat where Miles Franklin was to stay from May 1931 to September 1932. With this move the days of frequent relocation were over for Mary and Mabel; 181c was to be their home for nearly a decade until war and illness again disrupted the household in 1939.

Mabel Singleton once told Mary's sisters that her friend was 'a terror for London'.[23] A series of professional photographs of Mary Fullerton taken by the Kay Vaughan Studio there in about 1930 reveal a woman who has learned to wear her fine-boned austerity with grace and elegance. Gone is the awkward, shy demeanour of the earlier photographs; gone are the unflattering clothes, the big hats that threatened to crush the slight figure beneath them, the curls that made a futile and incongruous attempt to soften the thin-mouthed face. This woman with swept-back white hair looks confidently at the viewer from behind a pair of understated round glasses held in place by a fine cord around her neck – like a monocle but with two lenses, no doubt there to accent the intellectual quality of her serious face, framed by a luxuriant upturned fur collar. Still severe, yes, but emanating an assurance that has come with her new life in London, a sophistication that she never thought she would possess.

The Australian woman who had long before devoured books by English writers in her wash-house study at Glenmaggie in country Victoria thrived on the intellectual and artistic delights that the city of London offered her. With Mabel, who was frequently given tickets to the theatre by the "ladies" who patronised her business, Mary saw the plays of Shaw, Chekhov, Shakespeare and Ibsen, as well as the latest London farces like *Baby Cyclone*, a 'skit on the dog mania'.[24] They saw new plays by women too, such as G. B. Stern's *The Matriarch* and Clemence Dane's *Mariners*. (Mary noted to Miles that *Mariners* 'comes off quickly after tonight' because 'the men critics ... can't get the bias out of them, they don't realize it's there but it is regarding women's plays and other "works", they feel grudging to Clemence, feel uncomfortable that she isn't pushing a pram along the Broad

Walk'.)[25] Denis often accompanied his mother and Mary to the cutely-named Kensington Kinema in the mews behind their building where they took in the latest on offer in films. They went to recitals and concerts, galleries and museums; Mary also often attended literary lectures, including those given by Ethel Smyth and Vera Brittain about their autobiographical writings.

The journalist in Mary gave her a particular passion for tracking down the birthplaces or graves of writers and artists. She spent many days traipsing around London on such pilgrimages and now and then travelled further afield – to the birthplaces of Wordsworth, Tennyson, Wolfe and Milton, to name a few. She sometimes travelled alone but often combined holidays with Mabel and Denis with research for newspaper articles, such as those she contributed to the 'Great Men' series published in the Melbourne *Argus*. An article on Jane Austen's homes was also published in the *Argus*; other articles on women such as the English poet, Charlotte Mew, and the convict, Margaret Catchpole, remain as unpublished typescripts in her papers.

As well as combing London for material for articles, Mary found time to write two novels about Gippsland during these years, *The People of the Timber Belt* (1926) and *A Juno of the Bush* (1930). *Juno*, in particular, received very poor notices and she was mortified and outraged by the review in the Melbourne *Age*, which stated baldly: 'The author cannot construct a plot; nor depict lifelike characters'. (One criticism that it's fortunate Mary didn't know about came from Australian literary critic, Nettie Palmer, who wrote to her writer husband, Vance Palmer, of *Juno*: 'It makes me ache, to realise that her novel was so bad that the best I could do for it was to say nothing'.)[26]

Her non-fiction book, *The Australian Bush*, was published in 1928 as part of Dent's Outward Bound series. Mary also worked diligently on a pioneering saga about Victoria that she felt would complement Miles Franklin's Brent of Bin Bin novels set in New South Wales, but never found a publisher for *The Pioneers of Glendonald*. Finishing the manuscript for a crime novel in 1929 that was to be eventually published in 1932 as *Rufus Sterne*, she noted to Miles Franklin: '429 pages of quarto, about 130,000 words'.[27]

When I list what Mary Fullerton wrote during these years in London, I am aware of the sheer prodigiousness of her output. It seems that in spite of often poor health, frequent moves, a precarious financial situation and dubious critical reception, this was a highly productive period of her life. An undated poem written to Mabel, probably when the two friends were still in Melbourne, looks forward to a time when the instability and flux will be over and they can grow old together. Perhaps their new life in Letchworth and London in the 1920s was the beginning of the time Mary dreamed of in 'Somewhere':

> O, somewhere down the swift-increasing years
> That compass me like some still rising tide,
> When youth lies long forgotten, and the fears
> Born of her innocence are set aside.
>
> Then I shall find what now I cannot hold, –
> Your confidence, your dear delightful mirth,
> And all the intimate things we have not told,
> The joys that lift our spirits to Heaven from earth.
>
> When I shall see the well-remembered face
> Less clearly, and the dear head bowed more white,
> When Life's ambitions fade before Love's grace,
> And all misgivings vanish with the night,
> Our seeds of understanding shall have grown,
> And blossomed, in a garden all our own.

MEETING MILES

Mary Fullerton and Miles Franklin met in London soon after Mary arrived in England from Melbourne. Exactly when the meeting took place is not known, but a letter Mary wrote to Miles in April 1941 indicates that it may have occurred some time during 1922. In it she recalls: 'It is about 19 years since I first saw you. I'd your Town Planning address from Alfred Henry [Alice's brother] and called one day when up from Letchworth. I remember how cordial and undoubtedly pleased you were to see me. I was surprised [by] the very clear blue eyes looking at me and the warmth of your greeting'.[1]

Miles had been based in London for several years by the time she met Mary Fullerton. Arriving in war-torn Europe from Chicago in 1915, she made her own contribution to the war effort in 1917 when she spent six months in Macedonia with the American unit of the Scottish Women's Hospitals for Foreign Service. The unit was headed by Dr Agnes Bennett, an Australian who had been the first woman to receive a science degree with honours at the University of Sydney in 1894. Unable to find professional work in Sydney because of her gender, Agnes Bennett borrowed money to undertake a medical degree at The Medical College for Women in Edinburgh. Before Miles left for her war service in Macedonia, she wrote to Rose Scott in Melbourne, commenting 'I expect you & Dr [Mary] Booth both know Dr Bennett very well'.[2] Mary Booth had in fact been one of two young Australian women who had studied with Agnes Bennett in Edinburgh. My information about Dr Bennett comes from her 1960 biography, written under her auspices when she was in her late eighties. Given these circumstances, it is not surprising that it includes an example of what has been described as the *cherchez l'homme* tactic, common in biographies of single women. A woman who never married and who spent her life in the company of women, the only mention of a romantic attachment for Agnes Bennett occurs when her biographers claim that she fell in love when at Sydney University and probably would have married, but 'the young sailor', who remains unnamed, 'was accidentally drowned'.[3]

Miles Franklin returned from her war service experience to London in February 1918, taking doses of quinine for the malaria she had contracted. She said she was feeling more at war in the air raids there than she had in Macedonia where, ironically, she was 'far and safe from war's alarums'.[4] In September of that year she started work as a secretary at the National Housing & Town Planning Council in Russell Square, Bloomsbury, where Mary first met her.

During her life as a feminist activist in Chicago, Miles Franklin was in contact with many "New Women" who lived in partnerships with other women, although they, like Mary Fullerton, did not identify themselves in the emerging medical discourse of lesbianism. Jane Addams, the founder of Hull House in Chicago, was one influential woman who shared her life with a female companion; her relationship with Mary Rozet Smith spanned forty years. Described by Verna Coleman as 'Rose Scott writ large, on the grand Chicagoan scale',[5] Jane Addams introduced Stella Franklin into her circle when she arrived in 1906 with her letter of introduction from Vida Goldstein. It was there the young Australian woman first met her friend and mentor, Alice Henry.

In October 1907, Miles was invited by the dynamic national president of the Women's Trade Union League, Margaret Dreier Robins, to 'take care of what I term my correspondence and work'.[6] During the years she spent in Chicago, Miles worked her way up from part-time to full-time secretary of the WTUL, then to assistant editor of the league's journal, *Life and Labour*. In 1913 she became co-editor of the journal with Alice Henry. By 1915, the league was in disarray as a result of financial pressures and internal dissension; with the outbreak of war in 1914 Miles also found herself to be an alien in America, a position which no doubt caused her to think about where her allegiances lay. She was not yet ready, though, to return to Australia and eventually left America for England in October 1915. Even a month before her departure she was undecided whether to go to war-torn

London and risk a German invasion or to plump for the safer California. But as she wrote to a friend in Australia, 'The call of the blood is very strong and London lures me'.[7]

It was thought for years that Miles had concentrated solely on her political work in Chicago, but manuscripts that eventually came to light show that she continued writing during those years.[8] Many still remain unpublished, while one novel about Chicago that bears the name of the street in which the WTUL headquarters were situated, *On Dearborn Street*, was published many years after her death, in 1981.

A particularly curious finding was a novel that was brought out in 1915 in England under the authorship of Mr & Mrs Ogniblat L'Artsau by the romance publisher, Mills & Boon; *The Net of Circumstance* has only been recently recognised as being by Miles Franklin, the pseudonym based on her birthplace read backwards. This novel explores many of the writer's own preoccupations concerning sexuality, maternity and women's independence, and its heroine, Constance Roberts, shares parallels with Miles herself. It covers two years in the life of this single career woman in Chicago as she negotiates three offers of marriage by men who in various ways require her to compromise her principles. After a nervous breakdown, she accepts the man who expects the least compromise. Miles Franklin suffered severe depression that could be described as a 'breakdown'; she also had several romantic liaisons during the Chicago years but, unlike Constance Roberts, she remained single.

Miles, now forty-four years old, left London in 1923 for her first trip back to Australia in seventeen years, spending six months there with relatives and friends. It must have been quite a homecoming but, although she was welcomed by her family and saw old friends like Rose Scott and Dr Mary Booth in Sydney and Vida Goldstein in Melbourne, it appears her feelings towards Australia at this time were characteristically ambivalent. She wrote to Mrs Robins in the United States that the country had stagnated after the 'wonderful lurch ahead in all progressive laws and women's advancement' twenty years before.[9]

Miles's feelings for her mother were also ambivalent. Unlike the affectionate and uncritical relationship she had with her father, the bond between mother and daughter was complex and difficult. Miles Franklin's first biographer, Marjorie Barnard, described Susannah Franklin as a 'termagant . . . one of these Victorian women who carried the virtues of virginity to excess'.[10] Although she was to take on the role of dutiful daughter in later years, caring for her mother for five years until her death in 1938, Miles's ambivalence is indicated in the letters her mother wrote to her after she left Australia on this occasion. In one that Susannah Franklin wrote to her 'dear little girlie', she says rather wistfully, 'Whilst here I did all in my power to make you feel somewhat happy but often had a feeling that you were miserably disappointed with the whole thing, & wished you had never come, & I would often have loved to have taken you in my arms & kissed you, but you seemed averse to any affection'.[11]

By May 1924 Miles was back in London, working again at the Council and organising an international congress on women and housing. She had also gathered inspiration from a trip back to the Monaro region for the epic Australian saga she was planning to write.

Grounded in the nineteenth century in age and in their experience of rural colonialism, Miles Franklin and Mary Fullerton were embarking on new stages of their writing careers in the 1920s following lengthy periods of involvement in feminist activism. In Miles's case, a second novel had been published under her own name in 1909 – *Some Everyday Folk and Dawn*, set in Penrith (called Noonan in the novel) in 1904. Written before she left for America, the character of women's activist, Ada Grosvenor, was apparently based on Vida Goldstein, who had stayed with Rose Scott in October 1904 when she visited Sydney to give a series of lectures there. When this novel was eventually published by Blackwood of Edinburgh, it received a lukewarm critical response, totally unlike the furore created by *My Brilliant Career*. We know now that Miles had continued to write secretly during the Chicago years too, but she was still remembered principally for the novel she had written at twenty.

Miles had aspirations as a playwright while in London but

her efforts came to nothing in that direction, even though she was involved with the Stage Society which put on plays that were unlikely to receive attention by the larger commercial theatres. (*Old Blastus of Bandicoot*, the humorous romance novel that came out under Miles's name in 1931 had started life as a playscript that she gave Mary to read in early 1927.)[12] But the most important new direction Miles Franklin's writing was taking when she lived in London in the 1920s, far from the rural Australia of her childhood, was her work on that pioneering saga eventually to be published under the name of Brent of Bin Bin.

The first surviving letter of the hundreds Miles Franklin and Mary Fullerton wrote to each other over the next two decades is dated 'June 10th 1924'. Miles wrote to Mary in Letchworth from the Town Planning office to tell her how much she enjoyed *Bark House Days*, which Alfred Henry had given her as a parting gift when she left Australia. She also apologised for not being able to receive Mary when she had called at the office one day: 'I'm sorry I had to shoo you off the doorstep that day but I had a committee of 25 common birds like Orpingtons and Plymouth Rocks, and Red Game in full cackle and rare birds like a kookaburra or lyre bird could not be enjoyed then'. Miles's playful bird metaphor and her description of *Bark House Days* as like 'gum blossom honey' are early indicators of how important a part the fact that they were both Australian women writers was to play in this friendship.[13]

The slightly condescending tone of Miles's description of Mary's book as 'that sweet little book with its sweet little brown cover and its sweet little bark house drawing' also sets the particular dynamics of the friendship as far as writing was concerned. Mary, who understood and acknowledged that her prose writing lacked the scope of her colleague's, gave Miles unfailing support over the years in the writing of her pioneering novels, helping to allay the doubts and depression from which Miles suffered. She was also one of the few who were privy to the secret of the Brent of Bin Bin pseudonym. In England, Mary provided the crucial link between Miles and her publisher in Edinburgh, maintaining Brent's anonymity. Miles, in her turn, felt that poetry (which she did not write at all) was the medium most suited to her friend's talents. She worked diligently in Australia to get Mary's poems published, finally succeeding with the publication of two volumes in 1942 and 1946 under the pseudonym of 'E'. All in all, it was a happy arrangement in which the two friends' talents were different enough to complement each other and to obviate the competitiveness that undermines many literary friendships.

The relationship between Mary Fullerton and Miles Franklin developed gradually. After Mary moved to London from Letchworth in 1925, the two women visited each other for tea and brought pages of manuscripts out of their bags to leave for the other to comment on. Sometimes they read aloud from their work. Miles records frequent reading sessions in her diary, such as this one on 19 July 1926: 'Wet day. Took M E Fullerton home in a cab. She read me her play and manuscript entitled "In the Proper Order" and we ate big gooseberries'.[14] Occasionally Miles was less than generous to her friend in the privacy of her diary: 'Bad head. Mary Fullerton came to lunch and stayed too long'.[15] By early 1927, Miles was reading regularly to Mary from the manuscript that was to become the first of the Brent of Bin Bin novels to be published, *Up the Country*. Her listener was receptive, as this entry indicates: 'In afternoon went to Mary Fullerton and read some of old time novel and stayed till 10pm. She most encouraging. An epic of Australia never done before. Can she be right?'[16]

By the time Miles made her second journey to Australia in mid 1927, the manuscript of the first Brent of Bin Bin novel, *Up the Country*, was in the hands of her Edinburgh publisher, Blackwood. By this time, she and Mary had hatched the plot of her pseudonym together, the persona that was to both liberate and haunt the woman who wrote under it. Miles included a handwritten insertion marked 'Private' in a letter she wrote to Mary on the *SS Barrabool* just as she was about to arrive in Sydney via a stop in Melbourne. Referring to 'the glad secret we have up our sleeves', she gloats to her friend: 'I grin. I grin. You grin too and be werry-werry careful. Even if people suspect correctly we'll brazen it out and I'll escape, on to the high seas with Mrs Watson or up country with the 'possums or something'.[17] Brent of Bin Bin, the crusty old bearded squatter and story-teller, was born and Miles's desire to pose 'as a bald-headed seer of the sterner sex', which had been thwarted by Henry Lawson in the publication of *My Brilliant Career*, was about to be fulfilled.

On a more prosaic note, Miles added a handwritten note at the bottom of the letter: 'The biscuits were a great standby and at first I regretted you and Mrs Singleton spending so much unnecessarily but as the voyage advanced I blessed you again and again'. During her stopover in Melbourne, Miles said she had had many inquiries about 'Mrs S' and how Denis had grown up. She tells Mary, 'I said "a real beauty – a lovely crea-ture" and folks said that is how he promised'.

Miles Franklin kept a notebook in her later years in which she recorded pithy epigrammatic comments; these often refer to the differing natures or social positions of men and women. Typical of the comments about men is this: 'Men are perhaps logical in trying to exclude women from professions and work, because they are so sex-ridden that they are never sober in the presence of young women'. But another refers to women's sex drive: 'If women cd become free of physical lust at 25 or 35 instead of at 45 or 50 it wd be an advantage'. Miles never married, believing that the combination of marriage and career was an impossible one for women: 'A man's career is supported by his mother, aunts, sisters and often by his wife and mistress. A woman's career is attained in spite of father, mother, sisters and brothers and comes to an end in her husband'. [18]

Although Miles shared Mary Fullerton's belief that men were driven by their sexual inclinations and that society sanctioned this situation to the detriment of women, she also acknowledged that women too, including herself, experienced 'physical lust'. Unlike her friend who regarded herself to be 'asexual', Miles took on a resolutely celibate, but heterosexual, stance. According to her writer colleague and biographer, Marjorie Barnard, Miles remained an 'embattled virgin against the whole sexual world' all her life.[19] Even if we acknowledge that the prevailing ideas on the morality of sex outside marriage were much stricter than they are today, it is still curious that both Miles and Mary constructed their "chastity" as such an important feature of their lives. To begin to unpick this knot, I believe we need to broaden the specifically sexual arena in order to look at their liminal position as Australian women writers.

THE CHASTITY KNOT

The friendship between Mary Fullerton and Miles Franklin was conducted to a large extent through the medium of the written word, perhaps a fitting one for two writers. Their letters criss-crossed the world during Miles's second trip to Australia between 1927 and 1931, then the two women corresponded frequently from Miles's final return to her homeland in 1933 until Mary's death in 1946. In these letters they often referred to their writing in terms of childbirth, playing with the metaphor in colourful ways and with affectionate irony. In 1929, when Mary finished typing the manuscript of her novel, *Helen of the Headland*, (published as *Rufus Sterne*) she wrote to Miles: 'One can't judge and a mother looking at the crinkled face of her new born thinks him beautiful, sometimes he is so, sometimes not. One can't tell but I have put a lot of myself into this child'.[1] Miles, knowing her friend's reluctance to revise her work, replied urging her not to 'spoil this child for a haporth of milk in the composition'. In the same letter, she mentions a lecture that is to be given to the Lawson Society about Mary's writing, commenting 'that is a little layette for the child'.[2]

The childbirth metaphor is a favourite one for writers to use about their literary creations; indeed the magazine of the Melbourne Literary Club of which Mary Fullerton was one of the few female members bore the title, *Birth*. For *women* writers of the nineteenth and early twentieth centuries, however, this metaphor had a particular relevance beyond its general applicability to any creative act. According to the way knowledge had (and still has, to a large extent) oppositional associations that favoured men – man equals mind, woman body; man is active, woman passive, and so on – it was men's prerogative to give birth to ideas. In art and literature men were the creators, women the creations. Women's activity was confined to the body in the literal act of reproduction and, even there, they were perceived at least partly to be vessels for producing the creations of men. Those women who trespassed beyond well-defined limits onto male ground as serious artists risked moral censure as masculine, putting their respectability and their very status as women in jeopardy. By the early 1900s, with the advent of psychoanalysis, the favoured explanation used by critics of women writers became sublimation of the maternal instinct rather than a generalised masculinity.

In spite of this, there *was* a place for women writers in the contemporary rhetoric on motherhood, even if it was a marginal one and one that was usually expounded by women. A letter in *Australian Woman's Sphere* in 1903 outlined women's motherhood options succinctly: for most women the 'deepest and highest call in nature' was for wifehood and motherhood, but a minority were called to be 'mothers of the race' and fulfil themselves in social work.[3] Mary Fullerton aligned herself clearly with the second option in her capacity as an "advanced soul". There was a third option too, one that was taken up by both Mary and Miles; this lay among the small minority of women who were called to literary and artistic work and needed the unmarried life to produce their artistic "children".

That such a position was still regarded as inferior to literal motherhood Miles Franklin and Mary Fullerton vehemently disputed. Consciously and imaginatively taking up childbirth and motherhood – the activities that defined (and confined) women – they applied them metaphorically to the traditionally masculine realm of artistic creation. Thus, in their private correspondence, they attempted to take control of that imagery rather than letting it define them as second-rate mothers or as sexually abnormal or frustrated women. By using a metaphor that was legitimate for men to use about their writing and claiming it as legitimate but not identical for women writers' use, Mary and Miles were in the process of articulating a sexual/textual space for women, however tenuously,.

Yet legitimacy was still precarious. In *My Career Goes Bung*, written in 1902 in answer to the reception of *My Brilliant Career* but not published until 1946, the character of Sybylla Melvyn compares what she calls her 'spoof autobiography' to an illegitimate child: 'Those poor girls who have a baby without being married must feel as I did. There would be the baby but all the wild deep joy of it would be disgrace and trouble'.[4] Miles suggests here that women who wrote could only do so within certain boundaries for their product to be legitimate in the sense of being appropriately womanly.

Mary Fullerton wanted *The Pioneers of Glendonald* to be her 'child to Australia if not bone of my bone, something of my brain, however faulty'.[5] Written with this writer's usual modesty regarding her literary output, it is also characteristically ironic in tone, gently mocking the idealisation of childbirth and women's almost religious duty to reproduce. Mary's 'child to Australia' was pointedly to be a product of her mind. But although she contested the accepted oppositions of masculine mind and feminine body, Mary, who was also influenced by the moral codes of her time, had to take up the position of being "asexual" if she was to remain untainted by charges of illegitimate sexuality.

Although by the 1920s women were allowed a capacity for sexual desire that was not entirely bound up with maternal fulfilment, the links between these forms of desire among so-called normal women were still maintained. Single women writers were increasingly suspected of possessing an abnormally active sexual desire, one that was not directed – as in the natural progression – eventually towards the maternal. This hinted at lesbian desire in its construction as psychological *per*version rather than the masculine gender *in*version favoured by sexological theory.

When Radclyffe Hall's novel, *The Well of Loneliness*, was published in 1928, Havelock Ellis's construction of the homosexual as a 'congenital invert' burst onto the public stage in a most sensational way. Ellis wrote the introduction to the first edition of the novel in which the protagonist, Stephen Gordon, a self-confessed 'invert', pleads for the world's forgiveness for her hereditary flaw. Although the book is not remotely sexually explicit, it became the subject of an obscenity trial that ran for months and resulted in its' banning in England.[6]

Curiously, Mary Fullerton criticised *The Well of Loneliness* for its depiction of 'perversion' rather than the 'inversion' model that Hall used. Mary told Miles Franklin that she was surprised at *The Nation's* favourable review of the book in 1929, commenting that 'perversion' was 'in life . . . but so are some other things that art had best walk away from holding the nose'.[7] Perhaps, rather than picking up on Stephen Gordon's mannishness that was so unlike her own sense of identity, Mary was emphasising the actively *sexual* construction of the character who was, after all, a woman. Of the two, this element was far more threatening to her understanding of her own same-sex desire as non-sexual.

She implied as much in the same letter to Miles when she drew attention to 'a fifty-year-old spinster' winning a literary prize in London for a novel 'about a person who lacks the sex instinct'. 'I thought', wrote Mary to her friend, 'they would steer clear just now afraid of *The Well of Loneliness*. But of course the subject is as pure as the driven snow when not encompassed about with the psychos – not degenerate stuff'. 'There is the type', she concedes, 'and not necessarily depraved perhaps on the *up grade*, for we know not nature's ways or ultimate intention. Some have urged that all reproduction will become *immaculate* as the race advances, that these are simply 'advance souls'. I don't know where I belong except that I'm born so – that is that the process of reproduction is repulsive to me. I leave it there, though I could philosophise a deal, not time or room, my Miles. Anyhow I'm not a psycho case methinks'. Shades of Edward Carpenter? Plus a smidgin of anxiety about Freud, I suspect. I have not been able to discover the identity of this 'fifty-year-old spinster' who won the prize, but except for the discrepancy in the date, the 'type' Mary outlines here bears an uncanny resemblance to the narrator in her own prize-winning 1923 novel, *Clare*.

Mary separated art from life in her criticism of *The Well* when she referred to the things in life that art should shun, reflecting the belief that Art with a capital A carried with it a moral responsibility to uplift, one which had bearing on both Australian writers' negotiation of nationalism and sexuality. To women like Mary Fullerton and Miles Franklin, the responsibility lay in helping to "mother" a suitably uplifting Australian literature.

The nationalism of 1890s Australia was characterised by its masculine values, favouring stoicism, independence, anti-authoritarianism, mateship and physical prowess especially in relation to bush life. Australia's intellectual birth was the province of men, for the nationalist rhetoric produced a legend in which women were accorded little place beyond providing the new nation with its literal sons. Miles and Mary grew into adulthood in the 1890s and were highly influenced as writers by "birth of a nation" rhetoric, despite its implicit contradictions with their feminist beliefs.

Mary Fullerton's literary child was, significantly, to be dedicated to Australia. The already liminal and precarious position of women writers was exacerbated by Mary and Miles's colonial heritage and their investment in Australian nationalism. Nationalism and sexuality have been described as 'two of the most powerful global discourses shaping contemporary notions of identity'.[8] The depiction of the homeland as a female body has been deeply ingrained in nationalist rhetoric, dependent upon on a particular image of woman as 'chaste, dutiful, daughterly or maternal'. Nationalism itself, on the other hand, has been typically constructed as a male fraternity, a 'passionate brotherhood'.[9] This was particularly evident in the Australian nationalism of the 1890s, where the white male subjects were also colonials, traditionally situated in the space of the "other", a feminised space. The ethos of masculine mateship was strong, but so was the fear of its implicit, feminising homo-eroticism. To be manly was all-important, a priority that we are still familiar with in this country, at least anywhere beyond the inner-Sydney gay areas of Darlinghurst and Newtown.

It was inevitably a morally risky venture for women writers to claim involvement in this nationalist fraternity, situated as they were as objects in both nationalist and sexual discourses. The marginally legitimate space of artistic motherhood was one they could occupy, combined with the nationalist rhetoric of a new civilisation that was pure and fresh. Art could not afford to be tinged with the decadence they perceived to be rampant in the literature of the imperialist nations. As Mary wrote to Miles in

1928 about the new field of Australian literature: 'Women are the next top dogs . . . Such a field: consider its virginity, its scope'.[10] She echoes here the widely-held belief that women were not controlled by their sexual instincts as men were and who therefore, contrary to the masculinist ideal of nationalism, were more suited to developing the virgin field of Australian literature. Chastity was, above all, the legitimating factor.

Two related threads are woven through the letters of Miles Franklin and Mary Fullerton: their shared vision of a nationalist Australian literature to be led by women and their distaste for the growing prominence of sex and "morbidity" (covering perversion, madness and decadence) in the work of contemporary novelists and poets. The new nation was imaged as a strong and healthy young person, high-spirited but morally pure – a heady brew of theories of evolutionary progress, 1890s rhetoric that held the genuine Australian to be a product of the bush, and first-wave social purity feminism. The two women considered that colonial writers had a moral responsibility to reflect these ideals in their work, so they were particularly severe on women writers who failed to recognise this. Hence Mary's comment from London in 1929 on two new novels, Henry Handel Richardson's *Ultima Thule* and *Judith Silver* by New Zealand author, Hector Bolitho, both of which she contrasts with Miles's first Brent of Bin Bin novel, *Up the Country*: 'I am surprised', she tells Miles, 'that two of the Overseas books should have madness as their theme and so unrelieved too, not like a young new world to my mind but like the product of an old weary civilization. Your book is like a ride through the sappy bush on a spring day on a young colt full of life after these two books. Invigorating, yet you have not feared to make it of mingled yarn good and bad happy and sad as life is'.[11]

Miles Franklin echoed her friend's sentiments about decadence in her criticism of Barbara Baynton's experiments with bush gothic in the early years of the century, in *Bush Studies* and *Of Human Toll*: 'This sort of writing is termed powerful but its strength lies in sordid gloom and that is a pathological weakness'.[12]

The form of cultural nationalism constructing "Australia" as a pristine and virginal space to be inscribed by its intellectuals was a nostalgic vision by the time Mary and Miles met in the 1920s, its importance to them fuelled by their expatriate status. As time went on, much of their correspondence was taken up with railing in general against the increasing emphasis on sex in writing. By the 1930s, their own younger countrywomen were to come under particular fire. They saw the emphasis on sex and 'coarseness' in the writings of Jean Devanny and Zora Cross as a striving after 'false masculinity'.[13] Even their friend Katharine Susannah Prichard was criticised for having come under the influence of D. H. Lawrence, whom Mary thought was 'a passing and malign influence in literature'. (She did add pragmatically: 'it has done her no good. But it got her an English publisher'.)[14]

Mary and Miles's dream of the virgin scope of Australian literature was in the process of being sullied by the women they had hoped would lead the field, and they themselves were having a hard time getting their novels about pioneering Australia published. Neither writer, however, gave up her vision of what was to constitute the new Australian literature, nor did they alter their strict views on sexual morality.

It seems from her love poetry to Mabel Singleton that Mary Fullerton, at least privately, forged a woman-oriented cultural space for herself that was positive and able to accommodate her same-sex desire, even though its boundaries were always under threat. She became increasingly anxious about the "frigidity" label being applied to her poetry, for instance. In 1937, Miles Franklin confidentially reported Mary Gilmore's speculation that the poet "E" might be either Miles herself or a monk or a nun. Mary Fullerton's response was one of amusement tinged with worry as she expressed her concern to Miles that her 'nunnishness' might 'give the poems an appearance of *frigidity*'. She then continued: 'As for classing *you* as a possible, it is I think more of the intellectual possibility of the authorship for you are much more evenly human in nature on the sex points than I am, in short you are neither a nun nor a Puritan though you escape entirely the other extreme ... in short you are very normal in that respect I think'.[15]

Mary did not spell out to Miles that 'nunnishness' might have been a term that could encompass her love for Mabel, made clear in the poem she wrote so confidently to her lover many years earlier in 1912: '"Nuns fret not at their narrow cells"'. By the 1930s, however, domestic feminists like Marie Stopes and free-love advocates such as Dora Russell had taken up the notion that heterosexual intercourse was essential for a woman's mental and physical health. Frigidity was a new term that was closely aligned to sexual abnormality, one that hinted at lesbianism. Yet, in spite of her assertion that Miles was more 'evenly human in nature on the sex points' (heterosexual?) than herself, Mary managed to reconcile the contradictions between feminism and nationalism more successfully, I believe, than did her apparently more "normal" friend.

In her autobiographical writings – *Bark House Days*, *Clare* and 'Memoirs' – Mary Fullerton created her asexual but woman-oriented identity in part by taking up elements of the nationalist myth and adapting them to the feminist and socialist political beliefs she had held from an early age. She drew from nationalist discourse its depiction of the land as female, its egalitarian position on politics, and its commitment to mateship and the bush. Filtered through the lenses of her feminism and her predilection for women, the land became both a challenging source of strength and inspiration and an Arcadian space of female sensuality. She shifted the site of egalitarianism and mateship from the bushman to the figure of the pioneer woman, whose prototype was her own mother.

Often characterised as young and virginal in nineteenth-century literature and poetry, the Australian landscape was also represented there through quite contrary female images. Because of its harshness, unpredictability and resistance to male attempts to control and domesticate it, the land became metaphorically a whore or a dried-up hag. To the Northern European colonisers of Australia, Mother Nature was a benign figure; this new land was an unruly woman, a 'drought witch'.[16] Many women writers from widely varying times and cultures have, on the other hand, found the unruly woman to be an enabling figure rather than a threat. Mary Fullerton never found the land alien precisely because she saw it as both self-determined and sensual: Woman in her many guises.

Bark House Days, Mary's first piece of autobiographical writing, is the most nostalgic in tone, recreating more than any other of her works an Arcadian female landscape. In these sketches of her childhood in rural Gippsland – with titles such as The Hill, The Valley, The Creek, The Orchard, The Bush – Nature is imagined as a mystical presence to commune with and to learn from. Take this passage about the creek: 'In the cool shades of the ferny banks and their grottoes, under the fragrance of its beautiful wattles and young bluegums, with the 'love-in-a-mist' hue still about their tips, how many an hour have I lain and dreamed or drifted in that state, half-thought, half-feeling, which is as truly a time of growth as are the hours spent in toil or study. It was in those hours that I most belonged to her, and she to me; that whispering creek of many voices'.[17] Miles Franklin picked up, perhaps unconsciously, the female eroticism of *Bark House Days* when she described it to the publisher, George Robertson, as 'fragrant as a ti-tree gully with its creek lined with maiden hair'.[18]

The sensual Nature of *Bark House Days* becomes 'a tricky goddess' in 'Memoirs', the autobiographical piece that stresses the difficulties of life in the bush and explores the importance of the pioneer women.[19] The women who people Mary Fullerton's Gippsland landscape are middle-class women whose strength of character derives from their displacement from their English origins and their need to adapt to the harsher conditions of the new land and way of life in the colonies. In her depiction of these women whose friendships mitigate the hardships of isolated bush life, Mary gives the egalitarian mateship of the 1890s legend a feminist twist. Her mother is the central figure in this construction and the dimension of female friendship concentrated on in 'Memoirs' is the supportive structure that existed between the mature pioneer wives and mothers. This "mateship" mitigates the hardships of rural life, but instead of the adversarial relationship between man and the land in the myth, women and land exist in a relationship of shared adaptation.

The female world depicted in 'Memoirs' is a challenging space because of the Australian landscape's specific qualities. The combination of unpredictable female Nature and stoical pioneer woman makes an easy identification with the land impossible. They play off each other: identification, merging, sameness are lures, but difference continually reasserts itself, not the difference of the heterosexual male/female dichotomy but of a diversity of femaleness. This is reminiscent of the interplay of sameness and difference that lies at the heart of lesbian desire.

In her study of Australian women's autobiographical writing, Joy Hooton compares the negotiation of 'national and personal myths' in the work of Mary Fullerton and Miles Franklin.[20] She finds Mary's writing tolerant of ambivalence and sensitive to the dualities of the Bush myth: isolation and freedom, intellectual starvation and spiritual nourishment. I believe that Mary's characteristic fascination with dualities and her recognition that contradiction and paradox are not necessarily negative goes beyond a mere 'tolerance' of ambivalence to a celebration of it. This places her in a position of strength, enabling her to construct her sense of self in the spaces between conventional oppositions. At the same time she is forced to maintain her commitment to chastity and sexual purity or run the risk of being positioned on the abnormal side of the normal/abnormal sexual dichotomy. As a person, Mary rejected the categorisation of her same-sex desires as abnormal; as a nationalist writer such a positioning would have clashed with her investment in cultural nationalism and aligned her with the decadent products of what she perceived to be the "over-civilised" nations.

Hooton identifies, on the other hand, 'an unremitting polarizing impulse' in Miles Franklin's *My Brilliant Career*.[21] Opposites structure the work, negative mirroring positive – Caddagat's bountiful landscape and the barren plains of Possum Gully; Caddagat's library and the single book at the M'Swats' poor home. Against this background of oppositions that Hooton finds so pervasive that they assume the level of 'psychic metaphor', Sybylla Melvyn plays out her own mercurial mood reversals.[22] Her satisfaction, for instance, at striking Harry Beecham with a riding whip after he proposes to her turns immediately to horror at her action.

A further series of reversals occur in the scene – a mirror of the first – in which she teases her suitor until he grabs her so tightly that he leaves bruises on her 'soft, white shoulders and arms'.[23]

It is asserted that Sybylla's 'role-playing' in *My Brilliant Career* 'gives her the frail illusion of printing herself on a world that allows her no role'.[24] This observation could be extended to Miles Franklin herself who intrigued and puzzled all who knew her and who has continued to elude those who have attempted to write about her life and work ever since. Perhaps a clue to her enigmatic behaviour lies in her deeply ambivalent attitudes to all the things that were important to her: her family, her country, even her own sexuality. Whereas Mary Fullerton embraced ambivalence and contradiction, understanding that paradox underlies the dualisms that structure society, Miles Franklin resisted such uncertainties. Remaining enmeshed in binary patterns of thought, she railed all her life against the power differentials inherent in society's construction of masculinity and femininity.

The strategies Miles Franklin adopted to deal with these power differences paradoxically combined directness and evasion. She was, for instance, bluntly opinionated on matters of sexual morality and apparently open about her own sexual behaviour or, rather, lack of it. On the other hand, she deliberately cultivated herself as an enigma. One mystery that complicates the virgin story is the wedding ring that she is supposed to have worn on her return from America.[25] Her most obvious and extensive use of this strategy of contradictions is to be found in the complex web of pseudonyms she created for her writing. Some were used as authors of her novels, while the purpose of others was to deflect, or even create, suspicions by publishers and critics as to the identity of her major *nom de plume*, Brent of Bin Bin. These games of hide and seek led Marjorie Barnard to make the perceptive observation that Miles used mystery 'partly as display, partly as cover'.

Ironically, Miles herself was deeply committed to creating a unified self in the best liberal humanist tradition. She constantly attempted to evade awareness of the instability of her self-construction; she also displayed in her writing a kind of self-conscious awareness of her identity-making strategies that could almost be described as postmodern. In an early draft of her novel, *Cockatoos*, two neighbours comment on the character of Ignez Milford (who shares elements of Sybylla Melvyn and her creator). One says, 'She's one of the openest young girls I know', and the other replies: 'Quite! But if you try to get near her she closes up, very cleverly, with a seeming frankness'.[26] Miles Franklin here elucidates her own *modus operandi*.

Attractive in appearance and apparently flirtatious in the company of men, Miles established her heterosexual credentials early. Her performance of conventional femininity was evidently convincing; Norman Lindsay is on record, for instance, as remembering the young Miles Franklin for her 'pert rump' and 'alluring lips'.[27] But it seems Miles was aware that flirtation had less currency as she grew older. There is an element of bitterness in a letter she wrote to Mary in 1934, where she gives an account of her meeting with the mysterious poet, 'William Baylebridge'. Miles describes him at length, in less than complimentary terms. It appears that she felt slighted by his manner. She comments later in the letter that Baylebridge said she was not a bit like he expected: 'Always expected to see a huge woman with knives in her boots, because of the 'pungent virility' of my writing. Huh! Had I been young he would have fobbed me off with a 'virile' platitude about my glorious eyes and my long lashes, but as I was middle-aged he cd not forgive me for anything'.[28]

Miles had described him dismissively as looking 'like an American business man', but Australian literary critic, Nettie Palmer, noted in her diary that she found Baylebridge a 'strange, attractive character'.[29] One suspects that Miles would rather this fascinating man had complimented her on her glorious eyes than on the pungent virility of her writing. Her girlish, flirtatious behaviour was successful in creating an illusion of power in her relations with men only when she was young. Later in her life, her singleness and her lack of male partners became grounds for suspicion, as the suggestion of masculinity in Baylebridge's comment indicates.

Miles was often described as a 'filly' by male friends and critics. Even the obituary in *The Bulletin* for the writer who died at seventy-four contains these lines:

> Sprightly as a wild filly, she kicked over the traces,
> Stella of Brindabella, a brumby but thoroughbred;
> Refused to be yarded, curbed, driven or led . . . [30]

The analogy that praises Miles Franklin for her refusal to be 'yarded' (or in her own terms, 'caged') also pins her at adolescence, as a young horse who never qualifies for adult status as a mare. Sometimes critics' fascination with this unconventional woman has bordered on the prurient and her behaviour has been explained in the very terms she tried so hard to avoid: as sexually "abnormal".[31]

The sexual identity Miles Franklin created for herself seems to have been a reactive construction rather than a positive, enabling position. Formed in part to cope with the contradictions between the masculine egalitarian nationalist myth and her feminist desire for women's independence, it caused her to remain, at least in the eyes of many of her critics, a liminal figure like her heroine, Sybylla Melvyn, in *My Brilliant Career*.

CHAPTER TWELVE

181c HIGH STREET, KENSINGTON

Bloomsbury, where Miles Franklin had lived and worked in the 1920s, was a short ride on the tube from Kensington. It was an elegant area of inner London with buildings overlooking peaceful green squares where people walked and exercised their dogs or sat on benches under the spreading plane trees. The British Museum was there, housing at the centre of its warren of galleries the British Library – a favourite haunt of both Miles and Mary Fullerton. Bloomsbury was also home to an intellectual and artistic community that arose in the 1910s and flourished in the 1920s and '30s. The Bloomsbury group became synonymous with experimentation of all kinds – artistic, literary and sexual – and the name still resonates today through the works produced by the artists and writers themselves and, probably even more, because of the scores of books that have been written about their lives as part of the Bloomsbury phenomenon.

Bloomsbury is a place with rich associations for me. When I first visited London from Australia I stayed there, in an apartment overlooking Tavistock Square. Through the trees I could glimpse the building at the opposite end of the square that has replaced the four-storey brick terraced house that once stood at 52 Tavistock Square. Destroyed in the blitz in 1940, Leonard and Virginia Woolf had leased its top two floors from 1925, using the basement for The Hogarth Press and Virginia's studio.[1] Celie John, the Australian suffragist and close friend of Mabel and Mary, lived on the adjacent Gordon Square in the 1920s, her business address at the Dalcrose Society just a little further away in busy Gower Street. I walked through the rose gardens of Russell Square on my way to the British Library, close to where Miles Franklin worked at the National Housing & Town Planning Council and where she had lived in a small cold room with a gas ring for cooking.

The first time I went to work in the vast quiet of the domed reading room of the library, I trawled the long rows of reading desks that radiate out from the central information area like the spokes of a wheel, looking for a vacant seat. Eventually I found one and settled in with my folder of research notes. Looking up at the number engraved into the timber partition in front of me, I discovered I was sitting at seat s9, the only address Miles Franklin gave for Brent of Bin Bin. The persona she had created of the bearded old Australian farmer struck me as so incongruous with the physical surroundings of the library and the Bloomsbury ambience, I could not help laughing aloud at the thought of it, the stares from the readers around me relegating me to the position of gauche colonial that Miles and Mary were so familiar with.

The artists and writers who formed the loose-knit Bloomsbury group in the early part of the twentieth century came in the main from educated, upper-class backgrounds. Many of them followed the ideals of free love in heterosexual relationships, while homosexuality, particularly among the men, was common. Among the women writers and artists some, like the flamboyant composer Ethel Smyth, engaged in open relationships with both sexes. Others, such as Vita Sackville-West, referred to themselves as Sapphists, often remaining in rather unorthodox marriages while pursuing highly charged affairs with women. The sexually reclusive Virginia Woolf, who was loved at different stages of her life by both Ethel Smyth and Vita Sackville-West, once confided to her diary: 'These Sapphists *love* women; friendship is never untinged with amorosity'.[2] Others again, like Radclyffe Hall (upper-class but never really part of the Bloomsbury phenomenon) and the painter, Gluck, adopted the "invert" persona with panache, wore stylish suits and ties and had open sexual relationships with women.

Mary Fullerton passionately admired Virginia Woolf as a woman and for her feminist writing, particularly *A Room of One's Own*, but was critical of others of the Bloomsbury set as well as of their contemporaries such as D. H. Lawrence, whom she once described as a 'dirty-minded monomaniac'.[3] Writing on 'the sex mania rampant' among modernist writers, she explained to Miles: 'I blame psycho-analysis greatly for this but then the creative minds should never have succumbed to such strained application of a few facts. They had already lost Vision or would not have been dragged into the pit by Freud or anyone else . . . I say assuredly that one of Keates [sic] Odes is worth more than all the piffle, crude, rude and meaningless of the 'new poets' to whom the Bloomsburys of Europe have bent the knee'.[4] (Miles also admired Virginia Woolf's writing, but was less admiring than Mary of her person: 'I am surprised you think VW beautiful. In all the photos of her I have seen I think she has the real cold long colourless English face of caricature and to boot looks cracked'.)[5]

Mary regarded many of these writers to be intellectually pretentious and exclusive as well as rampantly sexual. In 'Outsider', a poem published in her 1942 collection, but probably written many years earlier, she satirises their snobbery and elitism:

> There was an awful silence once in Bloomsbury,
> That belongs to the catalogue of uncommon things.
> It happened like this:
> One evening in Lou Dunn's studio
> As we lounged on cushions on the floor,
> Or sprawled on Lou's divan,
> We talked of Art, and Life, and Love –
> All the things that people outside Bloomsbury
> Know nothing at all about.
> Suddenly a chap Harrington had brought in –
> A nobody somewhere from the Provinces –
> Chipped-in with a quotation – from Longfellow.
>
> Each looked at each,
> With the cold stare of conglomerate horror,
> Then, neither challenging nor pacific,
> Silent upon the freak with Harrington.[6]

Although women like Mary Fullerton and Miles Franklin thrived in the intellectual and artistic climate London provided, they also in many ways felt like "outsiders" in terms of class and cultural background. They were poor, sensitive to their marginalised position as "colonials" and imbued with the puritan attitudes of their rural Australian upbringing. As nationalist writers, they also associated the sexual experimentation of the Bloomsbury set with imperialism and the decadence of the privileged classes.

Respectability was a crucial part of their self-constructions. None-theless, London was Mary Fullerton's preferred home for the last three decades of her life, and Miles Franklin gravitated back there like a moth to the flame.

Miles Franklin was to remember affectionately for the rest of her life the fifteen months she spent at 181c High Street, Kensington, in the early 1930s. Based with her friend, Mary Fullerton, she got to know 'Mrs Singleton' better and also established a lasting friendship with Mabel's secretary, Jean Hamilton, who worked in the office beneath the flat. Writing to Mabel in 1936 from the family home in the Sydney suburb of Carlton where she cared for her elderly mother, Miles recalled her time at 181c with some carefully-crafted nostalgia: 'We were a great quartette. You and Jean so adventurous and game and undisciplined, and Mary and I so circumscribed by our Victorian and other inhibitions, and yet we were so breathlessly interesting to each other and ourselves that every day had its fun which far outweighed the bad madness of financial depression and so on'.[7]

I find several things striking in this account. The observation that the women were interesting to each other is commonplace enough, but the addition of 'and ourselves' points up the fact that the reciprocity of friendship can also heighten the process of fashioning one's identity. The interest Miles speaks of derives from both the similarities and the differences she identifies between the four women, coupling them in an unusual way but one that reflects her own specific focus. Mary Fullerton, whose primary relationship was with Mabel Singleton, she aligns with herself; in contrast to these two like souls she creates an "odd couple" out of Mabel and Jean Hamilton, who shared similar character traits, but who (as Miles well knew had a volatile relationship that often flared into open animosity. Finally, the 'breathlessly interesting' quality of the friendship network charges it with an almost erotic intensity.

In 1945, then in her sixties and living alone in the rambling family home in Carlton, Miles kept bantams, grew vegetables and made jam as though she were still a country woman. She confided in a letter to Mabel: 'I am too much alone. I'm all right when I have a congenial friend. If I were near you and Mary and Jean I would be quite all right. Happy association blooms like a flower: we cannot pick it twice'.[8] Friendships between women are often complex and volatile, none more so than those among the group of strongly independent women at 181c High Street in the early 1930s.

In 1930, after three years back in Australia, Miles Franklin had become restless. Writing furiously on the Brent of Bin Bin novels, she was also looking after her parents who, she had already told Mary, 'have no understanding whatever of the things writers have to face'.[9] She was less polite about her situation in her diary, written in an obscure form of shorthand only cracked in recent years. While most of Miles's frustration was directed towards her mother in this private outlet for her feelings, an entry made only one month after her return to Sydney in 1927 implicates even her gentle father: 'Cannot live long in this awful atmosphere. Awful old people killing me by inches'.[10]

She determined to travel again to America and England, to revisit friends but primarily to try to find more publishing outlets for her work. Making the decision to leave was difficult, as she confided to Mary at the end of 1930: 'I wouldn't mind going around the world steerage and risking my very last shilling that I had put by if it weren't for the tug at my heart here with the old people. Father is very frail and just on 83 and Mother takes more managing, but of course the longer I delay starting the more delicate the problem becomes'.[11] In addition, the news from abroad was not encouraging: 'Letters from America are very cautious and chilling. I can see they think I come to swell unemployment and a wild goose chase – surely not necessary to go all that way in person, say they'.

Miles sailed for San Francisco on the *SS Monowai* on 22 January 1931, armed with her book manuscripts and a collection of Mary's poems to try to place with American publishers. Little success was to come her way with either despite her efforts, and by April she was writing, 'I guess I must soon leave here. Have not yet accomplished anything but contacts'.[12] In the same letter, she asked Mary to find her 'a small cheap top room near you when

I come, but not with you as then we would kill each other with a flow of interests'. Whether Mary was unable to find a suitably 'cheap' room or whether she simply persuaded her friend to stay at 181c, Miles took up residence there on 8 May 1931 after being met by Mary on her arrival in London. Denis, who had joined the Air Force and was often away, had given up his room for the guest; when home he slept in his mother's office.

Most days Mary and Miles worked on their manuscripts. 'I am writing this morning in the sitting room that being a sunny quarter . . . Miles is in her bedroom getting on with some proof reading', Mary wrote to her sisters in one letter.[13] As usual, Miles's diary was a place for her to record her annoyances; she apparently spent much time helping Mary to revise her novel, *Rufus Sterne*, not always happily: 'Worked all day typing 'Rufus'. Mary got in muddle with papers, and will never learn about typewriting manuscript margins. Too much for her. Won't polish stuff, thinks it good enough'.[14] Mary herself was well aware of her need for 'editing' and later praised Miles for her diligence with her own writing: 'The way you work at a thing till you get what you *want* – what you *mean* always excited my admiration. Some of those pages scattered over the floor in your bedroom here with the gummed on bits!'[15] Miles might have complained about her friend's lack of editing and typing skills but she also records days of traipsing about publishing houses, trying to place her own and Mary's manuscripts. In one month she took *Rufus Sterne* to five different publishers.

On their days off, Miles and Mary 'went prowling about London', visiting galleries and museums, strolling in Hyde Park or going to lectures.[16] Mabel sometimes joined them when she had time and Denis, who was now the proud owner of a car, occasionally took them for a drive in it. Often in the evenings Miles, Mary, Mabel, Jean and Denis, in various combinations, went to concerts, films or the theatre; Miles also attended political campaign meetings for the forthcoming elections, usually with Mabel. As well as following Labour's campaign, the two women once went to hear the Conservatives speak at Lime Road Baths, Miles commenting 'God, how dull they are!'[17]

The pace was hectic during these months. On one occasion, after describing yet another visit to the theatre, Miles records in her diary: 'I must rest or I will die'.[18] Going to the theatre was more of a production in the 1930s than it is today as evening dress was usually worn. In the 1940s, Miles wrote to Mary from Australia of a visit she'd just had from 'Kath Prichard' who had spoken about Mary and Mabel: 'She said Mabel was one of the loveliest creatures she had ever seen. And I told how everyone used to look after her when we went to the theatres together (in that black velvet, do you remember?) she was so distinguished-looking. Should have been a cabinet minister at the least'.[19]

In the mornings or evenings during her stay at 181c, Miles often walked in Kensington Gardens with the 'distinguished-looking' and health-conscious Mabel Singleton. The friendship between the two seems to have developed gradually and, certainly on Miles's part, with some ambivalence. She referred in her diary to Mabel sometimes as 'Mrs Singleton', sometimes as 'Mabel', sometimes using the name, 'Virginia', the origin of which remains a mystery. (The name seems to have started around this time: Jean Hamilton always refers to 'Virginia', Mary never except in the dedication 'To Virginia' in her 1942 collection of poems, and Mabel herself sometimes signed her letters to Miles after 1932, 'Mabel Virginia'.)

It seems that Mabel's outspoken nature and quick temper sometimes frayed the visitor's nerves, while at other times Miles appreciated her pragmatism and ability to take charge. Three entries written over a few days typify Miles's changeable reactions:

> *3 May, 1932* Mrs Singleton unbearably cross and madly talking about everybody. Wet day. Typed heavily.
> *4 May, 1932* Typed again. Shoulder hurting.
> *7 May, 1932* Shoulder terrible – Mabel rubbed it.[20]

Mabel's practical help was always appreciated. In early November 1931, when Miles received the news by cable that her father had died, it was Mabel who organised for Lena (Miles's aunt who was in London) to come immediately over to the flat. Miles was devastated by the news, recording in her diary: 'Just flat as if the light had gone out. I never remember my Dad saying an unkind word to me – such a blank I cannot bear'.[21] Mary was just about to leave for a visit to her niece, Sophie Jenks, in her new home near Worthing and wrote to her sisters: 'It knocked [Miles] over greatly. I was sorry to be going away just then, but it was arranged and I could hardly put it off again. However she and Mabel did a bit of outing in the evenings'.[22]

A particularly strong friendship was struck up between Miles and Jean Hamilton who, at forty-one, was eleven years younger than the guest at 181c. Writing to Alice Henry, who was then living in California, Miles described Jean as 'a great acquisition to my necklace of friends'.[23] Jean, Miles told Alice, was 'an Australian squatter person' who came from pioneering stock in Victoria's Western District and who had led quite an extraordinary life. As a young woman in the early 1920s, Jean Hamilton had worked as a librarian at the Book-Lovers Club in Melbourne, established and run by Vida Goldstein's sister, Elsie Belle Champion. While there she met the Oxford-trained scholar and anthropologist, Sir Walter Baldwin Spencer. Employed to type manuscripts for him at the National Museum of Victoria where he was the honorary director, she seems to have developed during this time what Spencer's biographer calls a 'discreet association' with the professor.[24] More than thirty years older than Jean, Spencer was married and a prominent and respected public figure. A portrait of Jean Hamilton, painted by the professor's friend, W. B. McInnes, hangs in the Hamilton Art Gallery in Victoria; it shows a striking young woman with auburn curly hair, brown eyes and an aloof gaze.

Jean Hamilton and Baldwin Spencer travelled to England separately in 1927, Lady Spencer remaining in Melbourne. For the next two years they may have shared the flat Spencer rented at 30 Charlotte Street in Bloomsbury, where Jean acted as his secretary, typing his last two books. In February 1929, they boarded the *Tudor Star* (described by Spencer as 'a cattle boat') for Cape Horn, Spencer shipping as Pursar, Jean as Stewardess.[25] Spencer wanted to follow the voyage of Darwin's *Beagle* and to study 'the fast vanishing and little known Fuegians'; Jean was to study the Fuegian women. At first, their work in Tierra del Fuego progressed well, but in early July the professor took ill and during the night of 13 July, with fierce winter winds thundering around their hut he died, Jean Hamilton by his side. Her diary records the almost insurmountable difficulties she encountered getting his body transported to Magallanes, Chile, for burial, after which she managed to bring his journals and scientific collections back to England. The published version, which is all that remains, naturally records nothing of her feelings about losing the man who had been her lover for several years.

Mabel and Mary had known Jean in London before the Tierra del Fuego tragedy and she had apparently worked with Mabel then too. In 1927, Mary had written to her sisters that Jean had invited her to lunch to meet 'Prof Baldwin Spencer', whom Mary found 'a fine man so simple in his ways and no put on at all' in spite of his being 'the greatest authority on the anthropology of the aboriginals and their customs etc'.[26] In August 1929, Mary wrote to Miles about what had happened, a letter that gives us some more insight into Jean Hamilton too: 'You would see in the papers of the death in Tierra Del Fuego of our friend, Prof Baldwin Spencer. Mabel had had a jolly letter from him only a fortnight before the news came. Jean Hamilton who used to be first at the Champion Library, then over here with Mabel, was with him. The trip was to result in a vol about the Indian tribes down there. Jean was his secretary in the compilation of the last two of the Prof's books on the Interior Blacks . . . Later with him Jean was to go into Central Aus to get closer into the lives of the lubras than a man could do . . . Jean has the unusual qualities for such a task – some *drawing* property of nature'.[27] By 1930, Jean Hamilton was again working for Mabel, as her secretary and right-hand woman in the domestic hiring business.

Miles spent much of her time with Jean during her sojourn at 181C, often taking supper with her at her studio flat at 84 Charlotte Street, where she sometimes stayed overnight. Her diary entry for 21 June 1931 records simply: 'Rose late and talked all day to Jean Hamilton'. The month before this entry she had noted: 'Read Jean Hamilton's book "Spencer's Last Journey"'.[28] Jean's manuscript did not get published, but part of her journal that recorded

Spencer's last days and the time following his death was included in a book of that title edited by two Oxford dons and published by the Clarendon Press in 1931, also containing Spencer's journal of the trip.[29] The preface indicates that the book was produced on the invitation of Spencer's daughter, Mrs Young, and in it Jean is politely thanked for her contribution. Jean had previously published four articles in the Melbourne *Argus* in 1930, under the heading 'Among the Fuegians'. When she was later invited to give a lecture at Oxford on her experiences in January 1932, Miles helped her prepare for it.

A few months after Miles's arrival in London, Jean acquired a most unusual pet: a monkey she called Peter. He was a great favourite with Miles, providing the inspiration for her 'light novel', *Bring the Monkey*, which is dedicated to Jean and Peter. At the beginning of December Miles records: 'Went home with Jean for supper and read part of "Bring the Monkey" with Peter asleep on chest. Home very late'.[30] Three days later she finished the novel 'in rough draft', an amazing feat in three months.

Miles often took Peter out for exercise, either alone or with Jean, and his presence always created quite a stir: 'I had charge of dear little Peter and took him to Gardens where he delighted a ring of people by turning three somersaults in succession with infinite grace, time after time, ending up on my lap as I sat on the grass'.[31] Her changeable moods are again in evidence, though, as on another occasion she writes: 'Crowds after me in Park very wearing, and the children are such little whiners if the monkey just jumps on them they howl and their parents are equally stupid'.[32]

Peter the monkey also features in the diary of Winifred Stephensen, wife of Australian writer, P.R. 'Inky' Stephensen.[33] In July 1932 Miles Franklin and Mary Fullerton were invited to a gathering of Australian literary people to meet the country's most revered expatriate woman writer, Henry Handel Richardson. There, Miles also made the acquaintance of Inky and Winifred Stephensen, a meeting that was to have long-lasting repercussions for her. In fact, her return to Australia the following September was partly due to Stephensen's plan to set up the Endeavour Press in Sydney and his promise to make *Bring the Monkey* its first publication. The flamboyant and somewhat eccentric Inky Stephensen recalled that meeting many years later in a tribute by the Bread and Cheese Club of Melbourne to Miles Franklin after her death: '"Not *the* Miles Franklin?" I gasped, then added "Smell the gumleaves!"'.[34] On an ABC radio program he related a different version in which Miles came up to him saying '"I'm Miles Franklin. Smell the gumleaves"'.[35] Winifred Stephensen wrote in her diary at the time, however, that 'Inky didn't know which was who [at the party] and immediately on leaving demanded to be told who Miles Franklyn [sic] was'.[36]

Later that month, Miles records going to Jean's where she had dinner with Inky and Winifred. The meal, Miles makes a point of mentioning, was 'cooked by [a] Jamaican black'.[37] It was an occasion for business as well as pleasure, for she continues: 'And we talked Australian publication possibility. Home at 12.30'. Winifred also recalls that night in her diary, noting that 'a pleasant coloured woman cooked and served'. She records too that she was bitten by Peter, commenting 'the monkey has some pretty ways, but a great strain on one's nerves'.[38]

Winifred Stephensen mentions many meetings with Miles and Jean Hamilton over the next two months. The morning after the dinner at Jean's, they all met in Hyde Park, the Stephensens with their dog, Jimmy. 'It was most amusing', she records in her diary. 'Peter would nip Jim's back leg and Jim looked most annoyed and surprised. Peter was like lightning, he'd nip and spring up Miles or a lamp post or a tree – He was on a very long lead – suddenly after a nip Jim turned on him, his hackle rose, and he growled long and loud and snapped – After that Peter nipped no more and they were good friends – The person who most enjoyed all this was Inky – We were followed by an assorted crowd as I've no doubt they thought us members of a Circus – but on a Sunday morning in Hyde Park are always many strange sights.'[39]

A couple of days later, Inky and Winifred visited 181c High Street. Winifred wrote: 'Inky and I went to Mrs Singleton's for coffee and to meet Miles and Mary Fullerton. I had met MF and

Mrs S before – Inky much liked MF said she was a poet'.[40] Plans for the creation of Endeavour Press were proceeding at this time, and in August Winifred noted that 'Inky agreed to give J[ean] H[amilton] a job if she raised her own fare and Miles was very pleased'.[41]

In early August Denis Singleton was taken to hospital with pleurisy. Miles was in the process of planning her return to Sydney via America and, towards the end of the month, moved to Jean's studio for the remainder of her stay so that Denis could convalesce in his own room rather than sleeping in the office. Mary and Denis left for a trip to Devon, in early September, which meant that Mary was not there to see her friend off on what was to be her final return to Australia on the 8th of that month. I wonder if she realised then that she would never see her again.

On 6 September, Miles, Jean and Mabel went to dinner at Vaini's in Charlotte Street and on the 7th, Miles's diary records: 'To bed – last night in Jean's studio and with dear little Peter'.[42] Jean and Peter took her to Waterloo the next day and Inky Stephensen brought red roses. Miles left England in poor spirits: 'Very depressed and neck hurting. Went on board in pouring rain. Rain. Rain'. The Stephensens departed for Australia a few days later.

When Mary returned to London from her three-week trip with Denis, she had to face the absence left by the departure of her friend. She told her sisters, 'I can't say how much I missed her coming back here. She was at Jean's when I left and it seemed like a second going away. The others had got over the first feeling of missing her'. With typical understatement, especially when writing to her sisters, she continues: 'We hobnobbed in the evenings especially – as well as at morn and at noon. *The Times* crossword seems more difficult without her colleagueship at it'.[43]

Miles's diary records a hectic time in America, visiting friends and old associates from her years of political activity there. She met friends in New York, took the train to Canada to visit her old friend, Editha Phelps, boarded the *Santa Fe* for Los Angeles where she met up with more friends including Alice Henry, all this time never once complaining about the weather or about feeling tired or depressed. She left America at the end of October and by the time she had reached home, docking in Sydney on 18 November, the ebullient mood of the previous weeks had dissipated completely. Her homecoming is recorded thus in her diary: 'Arrived in harbour after lunch. War ships in evidence. Reporters came on after me but I hid in First Class. They got me in Customs. I refused interview. Rotters will never publish anything I write. How am I to live? Mother, Lena, Mrs Morgan and Mrs McCarthy met me . . . Ghastly homecoming'.

From then on, letter-writing was to be the only means of communication between Miles Franklin in Australia and Mary Fullerton in England.

SECRETS

'If one could be friendly with women, what a pleasure – the relationship so secret and private compared with relations with men', wrote Virginia Woolf in her diary entry for 1 November 1924. The whole nature of women's friendship is a well-kept secret in a world that talks endlessly about relationships between the sexes. Mary Fullerton and Mabel Singleton had a secret dimension to their relationship, one that was invoked in the private poetry Mary wrote to her friend. Those who have written about Miles Franklin's life have puzzled about her sexuality and brought to light the scanty evidence of a few romantic liaisons with men. The importance of her friendships with women has for the most part remained a secret, partly because she herself wove a web of secrecy around many of them. This was especially the case if they were involved in the maintenance of her biggest secret: the identity of Brent of Bin Bin.

Secrets were a crucial part of the epistolary friendship between Mary and Miles; in fact many of Miles's acquaintances were unaware that they corresponded at all. Miles wrote gleefully to Mary when Vida Goldstein was visiting London: 'Had a nice letter from Vida departing in which she mentioned that "dear Mary Fullerton" wd be delighted to have my messages and to hear of me'.[1] And when Nettie and Vance Palmer left for England, Miles warned her friend: 'Give no secrets away. I gave no hint of our intimacy'.[2]

As well as the frequent long letters Miles and Mary wrote to each other after Miles left 181c High Street in 1932, Mabel Singleton started her own correspondence with the Australian writer. Miles also wrote 'company letters' to the three remaining women of the friendship network, often beginning with such affectionate addresses as 'My dearest ducks, Virginia [Mabel], Jean, Mary . . . '. But the devious Miles Franklin maintained yet another, separate correspondence with Jean Hamilton, one that was kept secret from Mary and Mabel. She addressed these letters to Jean's studio at 84 Charlotte Street.

Jean never did get the job in Australia that was promised her by Inky Stephensen in August 1932. (His Endeavour Press published *Bring the Monkey* in 1933, but his desire to found a national publishing house came to nothing). By January 1934, Jean was writing to Miles: 'It is such a sadness that I could not have come out and got rooms and given you undisturbed peace where you could work'.[3] Miles still kept some hope that her friend would come to Australia, writing in July that 'Virginia [Mabel] might hold the job open' if Jean came to see her family. Miles had just visited her friend's mother and sister in Melbourne: 'I told them that Virginia had said often and often that after you anyone else would be so flat that she wd not continue the business. I hope I said the right things and gave nothing to the wind that shd have been kept in the bag'.[4] But in November of that year Miles was more circumspect, probably as a result of her experience looking after her own aging parents: 'You are stronger and much younger and more daring than I, but to get down among relatives in Australia – be warned, my dear'. As well as the caution, Miles sent her friend a Christmas gift, 'a little ornament I got in San Francisco for you, thinking you wd soon be after me'.[5]

The aura of secrecy that permeated the correspondence between Jean and Miles is still almost palpable when one reads the letters. Jean breathes: 'I do wish I could will you over here – there is much to tell thee in secret'. She sends Miles a Christmas present in 1933 from 'Peter little spirit and me. Quite a secret present – so mention it not in letters to 181c, will you?'[6] In another letter she confides: 'Unless you write jointly to Mary and me I never mention hearing from you. I hear all your news to them at lunch table and dislike intensely discussing anyone's private affairs with all and sundry'.[7]

Complaints take up a great amount of space in Jean's letters: about her employer, Mabel Singleton, about Denis Singleton, and about life in general at 181c High Street. Miles seemed to receive the often quite vitriolic gossip with enthusiasm, even urging Jean on: 'I shd love to hear your version of Denis. Mary's is splendid. He seems to be getting on magnificently as he always does'.[8] Miles does not, however, indulge in criticism herself: 'You see I do not comment freely – if you forgot to burn the letter straight away, it might make trouble, and we must leave no serrated edges'.[9]

At the same time as Miles was receiving Jean's version of life at 181c, Mabel was venting her feelings about Jean in *her* letters to the writer in Australia, saying that her secretary was 'at times as trying!!! as ever'.[10] By 1936, the situation between the two women had deteriorated further and Mabel became more expansive in her criticism. She could also be quite perceptive in her assessment of the problems of two strong-minded women working together: 'Jean is going through much change mentally. I will not attempt to explain it to you; at the present stage whatever it may lead to, I find her less desirable than she was. It is a *very* great test for two people to be thrown together as Jean and I have been in the Office and two of such different temperaments. I have always been too domineering (through being thwarted of legitimate outlets!!) and Jean has never obeyed or "given in" to anyone in her life or even met anyone "halfway"!!!'[11] Mabel finishes the letter with a plea to Miles: 'Do not think me disloyal to Jean; she has been wonderful here and it is appreciated to the full but she has hurt me a lot this year and it is a help to say a word, just a whisper to you'. As with Jean, Miles did not engage in the criticism, but she did defend her friend with such comments as: 'Do you remember telling me that Prof S[pencer] said she was the nicest human being he ever knew? We all loved her'.[12]

The tone of the letters Miles wrote to Mabel is quite different from the conspiratorial quality of her correspondence with Jean Hamilton. At the same time as she was listening to Jean's critical gossip, Miles often recalled in detail to Mabel the joys of her time in London with the community at 181c. In one letter she describes at length a conversation she had with Mary's sisters in Melbourne: 'They were so anxious to know about you all in London. I told them of our glorious days together – Jean, Mary, you and I and Denis and Elsie [their domestic help]. I said the only snake in such a delightful Eden was a little financial cark but all the world had that. I described the lovely little flat (big flat rather) and its most enchanting position in the middle of London and the plays we saw and the beautiful meals we had – often by the help of the wonderful bargains Mary found in strawberries etc and the cakes she cooked and how we ran a school for geniasses upstairs while you and Jean ran a business for Duchesses downstairs, and how you said that sometimes in the enthusiasm you were not quite sure whether it was a fight that was going on between Mary and me, but that it was only fervor: and that you and Jean were the freebooters and Mary and I the ancient puritans . . . I am not wholly joking in the above classification. Mary and I are too steady for this gambling age. It wants the freebooting spirit to take chances. It depends on you and Jean, if you could exploit Mary and me. Jean has the pluck to shoot off into space after opportunity and you have the courage of Britannia to storm the citadel'.[13] The same letter, addressed to 'Virginia darling', also contains a rather back-handed compliment: 'Saw a photo of the young you at Arden, but it was in the days when we made such haystacks of our heads that it detracted from your beauty'.

Perhaps the contradictory mix that occurs in these letters is another example of Miles Franklin's ambivalent attitudes, but it is also indicative of the complexity of friendship networks. When I first started reading the correspondence between Miles Franklin and Jean Hamilton, I felt as though the ground had shifted beneath me. My initial impression of great harmony at 181c High Street when Miles stayed there was shattered by Jean's complaints about Mabel's domineering and garrulous nature, about Denis's 'airs and insincerity', and about the 'narrowness of outlook' at 181c.[14] (Perhaps sensing her limits with Miles, she hardly ever indulged in disparaging comments about Mary.)

On further thought I realised that the talk of married women when they are without the company of their men often turns to quite acerbic comments about their partners and about men and the married state in general. Complaining provides an outlet for frustration. Gossip, a close ally of secrets, has historically been associated with subordinated groups such as women. For single women who live and work together, the sense of community is often strong and sustaining; on the other hand, the inevitable tensions that arise from close relationships cannot easily be vented from within that community. It seems that Miles might have served as an outlet for both Mabel and Jean's frustrations; she knew the situation at 181c intimately, and yet she was removed from it. Her ability to be a secret sounding board is obvious. She also, given her love of secrets, clearly enjoyed the knowledge that she was privy to information of which the other parties were unaware. Miles's long-standing friendship with Mary Fullerton had its own dynamics, in which literary gossip that was often quite disparaging towards their colleagues was a constant feature through which they defined their own positions as writers. They never discussed the other two women's differences.

Virginia Woolf's novel, *Orlando*, has been described as a love letter to her friend, Vita Sackville West.[15] Although a work of much less significance, Miles Franklin's *Bring the Monkey* could be said to be her "love letter" to Jean Hamilton (and to Peter the monkey). Dedicated 'To JEAN and PETER in memory of variegated and heart-warming experiences', it is a spoof on the detective novel. The principal characters are two young women, Zarl Osterley, who distinctly resembles Jean, and the narrator, who is not unlike Miles herself. Zarl, a vivacious Australian with 'delectable copper-tinted curls', is described as resembling 'a champagne glass, not alone in grace of fashioning, but in effervescent contents. The bubbles are intensely fascinating'. She wishes to acquire a monkey because she is bored, 'just going to bed and getting up again'. Her friend replies: 'I should have thought you had enough of the sleet on the desolate bays of the Beagle Channel when you went to the Horn'. The narrator disguises herself as a maid (which Miles did herself as a young woman) and together the two friends and Percy the monkey attend a weekend party of stuffy English aristocrats and exotic guests on a country estate. They survive the extraordinary events that occur there to emerge at the end of the book with their friendship intact, Zarl having warded off several suitors, including an elephant hunter and an aviator.

Miles was clearly fascinated by Jean Hamilton, the woman who once gave a talk on BBC radio on the subject of being a 'female "rolling stone"', describing her 'inner urge' as 'an intense desire to touch life from all points'.[16] Soon after her return to Sydney in 1932, Miles had confided in her diary: 'Feeling very depressed. Wish I had some friend near to take and extend a little affection. Jean for choice'.[17] Their correspondence continued for several years, but in the late 1940s Miles wrote to inquire what had happened to her friend. 'Jean Darling', she begins, 'How are you or where and why and when? I note among some old papers that you sent me a cable for 1946 and I believe that is the last whisper I have had of you. When I sadly had to leave you I said I expected few letters because you were always so engaged charming and being charmed that you did not go into dull corners and write as the natural born correspondents do . . . For a time you astonished me by sending grand letters. And I had those photographic ones during the war but now when the holocaust has swept past leaving you safe and sound – not a word from you'.[18]

To Jean's reply, Miles responded: 'I see that your unafraid spirit of adventure and personal charm are still all there to go out from the ground up to tackle making a new start . . . No wonder you have no time to read books. Don't need to when you are living life so fully. I wish I was there near you to touch it sometimes'.[19] The correspondence continued sporadically until 1954, Jean's handwritten air letters becoming almost impossible to decipher.

According to Miles, Jean's 'heroic friendship for the Prof' was the 'keynote' on which she built her respect for her friend. 'My respect for you', she added, 'gets somewhat overlaid by my affection which is so easy where one party is as charming and kind as you, and the other as affectionate as I am'.[20] But there was another reason for the separate correspondence Miles maintained with Jean Hamilton. After 1932 she involved her as a new go-between in the Brent of Bin Bin secret, largely supplanting her staunch friend, Mary Fullerton.

In early 1933, Miles was still negotiating with Mary over unpublished Brent manuscripts that were in her possession and stored at 181c: 'Please post enclosed without delay. I enclose copy of letter which will save explanation and which will keep you informed. In case I shd have to cable, I shall call COCKATOOS,

BIRDS'.[21] Mentions of the Brent intrigue then fall away and Miles concentrates on her efforts to get Mary's poems published in Australia (keeping the poet's identity secret of course). In accounts of her own work she was pessimistic, as in this letter written in 1934: 'I really am in a dark long lane with no turning except senility and old age and utter poverty and there is no good of passing on depression and I am too weary to "buck up" any more'.[22]

It seems, however, that Miles's explanation of 'depression' may have been used at least partly to fob off her friend, that she may have planned to make Jean her main ally in her literary secrets. In December 1933 she had confided a new secret to Jean, that she was working on 'a big canvas novel of Australia', one that Jean was to dub her 'Mag Op'.[23] Right through that year she had been writing *All That Swagger*, which was eventually published under her own name in 1936. Early in 1934 she told Jean: 'I shan't tell any of my new business . . . Burn this as soon as read'.[24] There are discussions through 1933–34 about showing *Up the Country* to Robert Flaherty, a film maker, and *All That Swagger* to Guy Innes, an Australian journalist working in London. Jean appears to have been less than successful in her role and frequently apologises for not getting things done: 'I never seem to achieve anything for either myself or anyone else so you must not make me feel my own lack of ability and guts. I do wish I had more time – 10–6 pm leaves one no margin for any other business activities. You say, "if you will show it [*Swagger*] to anyone". I presume you mean publisher? I wish you had been more clear about this'.[25]

One reason for handing over the secret of Miles Franklin's 'Magnum Opus' to Jean seems to have been Mabel's inability to keep secrets, even though Mary had confessed in 1928 after receiving a copy of the first Brent of Bin Bin book: 'I told Mabel or she guessed . . . but mum is the word with her'.[26] But after staying at 181c, Miles was not convinced of that; Jean Hamilton was also there to constantly fan the flames of mistrust about 'Virginia's babbling'. Jean had also implicated Mary in the problem, telling Miles of an argument she had had at 181c: 'Mary threw the ball by relating her encounter with [Guy] Innes – Denis and his lass

Eileen Reid were also at lunch'. Jean relates to Miles that she told them that 'the only way to keep a secret was to tell no one and that I trusted no one and women were utterly hopeless in this way'.[27] Miles responded by writing to Mary asking her to 'sit tight' and resist the Australian journalist's questioning about the identity of Brent, adding diplomatically: 'If we don't get money in life there will be some fun in knowing what women could keep secrets when we go'.[28] She later reminded Jean to '[n]ever let Innes meet Virginia or she would give everything away in first breath. Just keep things in separate compartments'.[29]

Miles did not tell Mary about *All that Swagger* until 1936 when it won *The Bulletin* prize: 'Dearest Mary, July 24. Just a tiny note to tell you that I have been awarded *The Bulletin* prize for this year. I dropped into the competition a carbon copy of a long novel which I wrote in the beginning of 1933, immediately upon my return, and which has been lying about ever since'.[30] Mary was out of London at the time but her reply was instant: 'My dear Miles, Did you hear me whoop? The splendid news lifted me right into the air . . . Mabel got the letter and phoned me at once, she was quite dithery with excitement and delight'.[31]

In August, Mary received a note marked '*Very Private*' from her friend: 'Further to what I have said of Brent. Now is the time to keep the door tighter than ever, no matter what people say or prove. Perhaps Brent can finish his series now. Blackwood can be written to. If any letters come to Miss Mills c/o you, please grab safely and send to me'.[32] Jean's stint as Miles's unofficial "literary agent" seems to have been terminated and Mary reinstated. Whatever the discreet Mary knew of the situation she kept to herself. And the 'garrulous' Mabel never did divulge the secret of Brent of Bin Bin's identity.

Mary Fullerton's many pseudonyms can be traced back to more or less pragmatic motives associated with the bias against women in the fields of journalism and poetry. She was also sensitive to her lack of formal education and, later, to the bad notices she received for the novels published under her own name; after the reception of *Juno of The Bush* in 1930, she never published a book under her own name again except for the illustrated edition of the previously-published *Bark House Days*. The creation of Miles Franklin's Brent of Bin Bin pseudonym also had its practical motives, especially since she was a spinster with all the connotations that term carried. As Valerie Kent has put it, it 'freed [her] to write caustically and often bitterly of men, marriage, and motherhood without being accused of being shrill, unfeminine, or unnatural'.[33]

Beyond practical reasons, there is a major difference between Brent of Bin Bin and Mary's aliases such as Robert Gray, Gordon Manners, or even her *nom de plume* for her later poetry, 'E'. Whereas the pseudonyms chosen by her friend remain mere names (or initials, Miles Franklin's crusty old Australian squatter developed a three-dimensional quality that became almost flesh and blood. In one letter to Mary she relates a conversation with poet, Mary Gilmore: 'Mary Gilmore, who must be quite cracked, told F Davison [Frank Dalby Davison] that Brent had called to see her and that he is a big man with a red beard. I wonder did anyone call impersonating Brent, or did she make it up. It was told to me, expecting me to deride it, and of course just fishing – but I said seriously – 'I somehow never thought of his having a *red* beard'.[34]

Even her publishers were kept out of the secret and Mary became an indispensable intermediary in London, receiving and sending correspondence between the Edinburgh-based firm of Blackwood and Miles Franklin in Australia. As we know, Brent of Bin Bin gave his address as Seat s9 in the British Museum reading room, receiving correspondence there (again through Mary) and writing letters of his own to colleagues such as Nettie and Vance Palmer and "Inky" Stephensen. Many people suspected that Brent of Bin Bin and Miles Franklin were one and the same (indeed she constantly left deliberate clues at the same time as she was covering her tracks), but she never admitted to the authorship of the novels written under his name. She knew, however, that the suspicions would be confirmed when her papers became available after her death.

Why did Miles Franklin expend so much energy and time over many years to create and preserve the mystery of Brent of

Bin Bin's identity? P. R. Stephensen dismissed it as 'a spinsterish whim' and 'feminine foolishness';[35] Marjorie Barnard concluded more perceptively that Miles's secrecy about her pseudonyms and her silences about periods of her life 'all point to some deep hurt'.[36] While the complex nature of the creation cannot be reduced to a single cause, I believe the emergence of the Brent of Bin persona was one of Miles's attempts to cope with what she perceived to be the irresolvable masculine/feminine dichotomy. It was also an attempt to reconcile the contradictions between the discourses of nationalism and feminism: between the "virile fraternity" that espoused freedom but excluded women and the movement dedicated to women's independence.

Miles had found that to tread on what was considered male territory was dangerous when *My Brilliant Career* was published; even her attempt to combine the self-mocking form of the masculine and nationalistic "yarn" with a parody of the feminine romance narrative was disastrous, being read as 'bitter and egotistical'. What was manly from the pens of men was merely unwomanly when the writer was a young single woman. Sexologist Havelock Ellis, who made the above comment, also included a passage from the novel in the essay, 'Love and Pain', published in his *Studies in the Psychology of Sex*.[37] He quoted the section in *My Brilliant Career* where Sybylla laughs to find bruises on her shoulders from Harry Beecham seizing her by the arms, saying it supported his theory that women – particularly those who were lower on the evolutionary scale – find sexual pleasure in subjection and pain. It is hardly surprising that the besieged writer took refuge in a male pseudonym!

Most importantly, the Brent of Bin Bin persona enabled Miles to pursue her revisionist project of defining an Australian nationalist literature: she could use the masculine epic form (which could also incorporate the bush yarn) in order to reconstruct in fiction the birth of a nation. And who better to write this saga than an old bushie himself?

The invention of Brent of Bin Bin also helped to preserve Miles from the kind of embarrassment she and her family suffered over the scandal of her first novel. How important the pseudonym was to her is made clear in a letter she wrote to Mary when the first Brent novel, *Up the Country*, was published in 1928. Miles told her friend that she felt 'like some cowering exhausted animal in an inadequate cover', agonising that she should have taken more thorough and efficient means of hiding her identity in order to prevent 'being tortured with personal publicity'.[38]

It is clear from the correspondence between Miles and Mary that the sense of freedom the Brent secret conferred on both of them helped to balance the problems they encountered with publishers and critics as women and as colonials. The sheer fun the two women derived from sharing the secret and contesting those stereotypes was empowering and formed a crucial component of their friendship. They shared a love of mystery and Mary entered thoroughly into the spirit, often doing detective work of her own.

While Miles' pseudonym freed her in some ways, it also had a converse effect. When she was about to leave for America in 1931 to try to get her work published there, Mary asked if she was going to reveal the secret of Brent's identity. The day after her arrival in New York Miles gave this extraordinary reply: 'No, no, I am going to say when tracked to my lair by circumstantial evidence, which is inevitable for lack of collaborators of trustworthiness, that I am acting as his agent, that the old toad owed me something for what I suffered through him. God knows that is true, I have suffered by, with and because of him all my life'.[39] What could she have meant when she said she had always 'suffered by, with, and because of' Brent of Bin Bin? Perhaps Miles Franklin was referring to Australian society's masculinism, which she felt had thwarted her personal life and her writing career. Although the creation of Brent of Bin Bin had allowed her to take on the role of nationalist pioneer, once her cover was revealed she would revert to being 'only a woman' as Sybylla Melvyn had cried at the end of *My Brilliant Career*. Instead of being a useful tool, the device seems to have taken on a life of its own and she became haunted at times by this persona who could turn into an 'old toad'.

Taking on a male identity did not help Miles explore her

female sexual identity, nor did the freedom it conferred on her extend to a modification of her rigid stance on chastity. On a practical level, to do that when she was also making sure people suspected that Brent was at least partly a creation of Miles Franklin would have been counter-productive. More fundamentally, the taking on of a male identity did not mean that Miles relinquished the moral codes she learnt from her mother and her late nineteenth-century rural Australian background. Historian, Jill Roe, has observed how pervasive concepts such as chivalry were in colonial society; what began as a ruling-class ethic in Europe became transformed in a society where 'perforce behaviour, not breeding, mattered most'.[40] Consequently, Brent of Bin Bin, who represents the idealised nationalism of the 1890s legend, is a bachelor but he is also elderly, putting him beyond the age of the "sexual imperative". While the figure of the single male, particularly if he was a thoroughly masculine bushman, did not carry the stigma of sexual frustration that attached to the unmarried female, it seems that Miles was in many ways still reworking the tapestry that featured the chastity knot.

Miles Franklin always wished to separate women's friendships from the slur of sexual frustration, which she equated with lesbianism in its most negative formulation. In 1944 she wrote to Mary Fullerton about an encounter with Marjorie Barnard, saying that she had defended Barnard and her co-writer, Flora Eldershaw, against 'aspersions of frustration and lesbianism'. She added that 'tho MB in particular has been so virulent to me I still will not countenance such depiction of a good friendship and smooth collaboration between these women'.[41] Miles positioned lesbianism and friendship as oppositional forms of women's relationships – one pathological, the other productive. This was a position not unlike Mary Fullerton's own. Miles could write this letter in the knowledge that her friend would agree with her defence of Barnard and Eldershaw, whose collaboration as novelists had made them leading Australian writers. Their agreement that "perversion" should not be involved in "art" is a fundamental cord binding Miles and Mary's literary friendship.

I found in Mary's diary clues to the books she was referring to when she wrote the poem, 'Biography', in 1940 as a reaction to 'reading some recent biographies':

> *July 6, 1940*   Reading Havelock Ellis, think he was a crank.
> *Aug 1, 1940*   Madame lent me 'Life of Brontes'.
> *Aug 14, 1940* Wrote rhyme 'Biography'.[42]

The Ellis book was the sexologist's autobiography, *My Life*, published in 1940, in which, Mary told Miles, he showed his 'bad taste' by, among other things, writing of 'his wife's "homo" affairs'. (Edith Ellis did consider herself an "invert"). She added: 'My conclusion is *doubt of the truth* of these things and feeling that he had a kink amounting to abnormality. The book made me hate him and the "sciences" he gave his life to, fumbling and fiddling about sex things most of it merely unhealthy and unsettling of the man's own balance'.[43] Miles wrote back agreeing about Ellis but, oddly enough, supporting Edith strongly: 'Yes, I always did resist Havelock Ellis's findings. He hadn't enough experience and give in him to make them right according to imagination as well as to scientific laboratory work. He was the delving mole trying to fly, and made a squawking mess. His burblings to poor Edith about his fancies when she was mad enough to love him so were egregious. We had her in Chicago when she was undergoing that torment, poor woman – and this gentlemanly revelation explains things she said. In those days of splendid experiment in breaking bonds some women tried to stretch outside their capacity and I think Edith Ellis was one, and I think she was very brave'.[44]

Many biographers of the period applied sexological and psychoanalytic theories to their subjects, and the Brontës (whom Mary was reading about in 1940) offered rich pickings. Much was made of Emily Brontë's so-called sex-frustration and "masculine" behaviour – codes for possible homosexuality – which so enraged Mary she told Miles 'authors of the bunkum should be killed no less'.[45]

Though Mary and Miles agreed about "perversion", there are differences in the ways the friendship/lesbianism distinction functioned in the thinking of the two women. One of the crucial differences was Mary Fullerton's belief in the evolution of the so-called advanced soul, a belief that underpinned her artistic and political vision and allowed for a view of friendship that could, in its highest form, incorporate same-sex desire. The 'loneliness of soul' that Mary aspired to involved a transcendence of hetero-sexual relations: 'We have a long sublimation to make yet but it is begun – beautifully begun', she told Miles. 'Love has left the jungle'.[46] The highest form of friendship between women, which Mary saw as being akin to heterosexual love at its best but without its inherent inequalities, formed part of that transcend-ence, while friendships with men were possible when sexual interest was not involved. While Mary's vision may seem arcane and idealistic (and also racist as the advanced soul was more highly-developed than the "primitive" races), it was in fact more accommodating to the material practice of her life than Miles's demands of women's friendship were to hers.

Miles Franklin's view of the inevitable loneliness of the woman writer appears to be based on a depressing vision of heterosexual incompatibility: relationships between the sexes were inevitably based on sexual power differentials whereas female friendship was a domain where these differentials did not operate. Histo-rian, Carol Lasser, has observed a 'sororal mode' to operate in women's friendships of the nineteenth century, one in which sis-terhood was idealised (in a manner not unlike the sisterhood ideal of 1970s feminism). It was one in which 'the expectation and idealization of harmony between sisters remained' even if 'rela-tions between sisters were not always cordial'.[47] Miles Franklin's conception of female friendship has resonances of this model; she seems to look back to a nineteenth-century idealisation of friendship to combat the twentieth-century threat of lesbianism. She frequently described Mary and Mabel's friendship as noble and, after Mary's death, urged her companion to write the story of their relationship: '[A] time may come when people will be as avid to know something about Mary as they are today to know about Emily Dickinson, and you have the power to supply that information in a memoir that can be kept till the right time. You must tell about your meeting with her, all that she meant to you then, and the last heroic years when you were more than a mother and sister in one to her. It is a glorious rare friendship, knowledge of which must not be lost to the world'.[48]

Miles situates this 'glorious rare friendship' within the familial model (which she also idealised), identifying Mabel as 'more than a mother and sister' but, by implication, less than a lover. Not surprisingly, she was shocked by a 1950s biography of the poet she compared to Mary, which depicted Emily Dickinson as a miserable and psychologically damaged lesbian. In a draft letter to a reviewer of the biography Miles observed (rather incoherently): 'In the 20s and 30s one could not enjoy one's friendships without this foul aspersion. I'm so glad that you point out that *The Well of Loneliness* terms do not fit Emily's century nor indeed my girlhood in every way and [we] were also well healthily able to live without 'Freudian' complexes of the freudians'.[49]

Mary Fullerton adapted friendship so that it could in some cases incorporate same-sex desire; Miles Franklin distinguished 'noble' friendship from 'foul' lesbianism. Constant policing of the boundaries between them was required and Miles reacted with typical ambivalence to the distance between the real and the ideal, oscillating between the two in apparently contradictory fashion. Mary's friendship with Mabel helped keep the ideal alive for her and Miles related the glorious friendship between the two women in glowing terms in her letters. On the other hand, Miles obviously enjoyed the gossipy and often nasty letters of Jean Hamilton.

By keeping her relationship with Jean separate from her friendship with Mary, Miles seems to have been able to keep the real and the ideal from contaminating each other and still hold up the life-long friendship between Mary and Mabel as a symbol. Her long-distance flirtatious relationship with the younger Jean Hamilton is also quite different from the tone of her letters to Mary Fullerton. It forms a slight chink in her exclusively heterosexual armour. But what Miles Franklin did not seem able to do was risk contaminating her ideal of friendship by entering into relationships with women where that fragile boundary between friendship and sexual relationship might have been tested.

'AN EXHILARATION OF TRAGEDY'

Two years after she returned to Australia in 1932, Miles Franklin wrote to Mary Fullerton suggesting that she should try to publish Mary's poems herself. It would be, said Miles, 'a life-saving adventure for us both and an historical flower of our friendship'.[1] Mary had sent her a collection of poems in early 1933 after they had been turned down by Blackwood and the Woolfs' Hogarth Press: 'Well you asked for the ninety-five poems and here they go', she wrote. 'Just loose – I have them all loose. So don't be frightened of losing etc. You may as well have them.'[2] The poet, however, declined her friend's later offer to publish them, saying, 'If you were rich it would be different . . . I thank you all the same and wish we could get the little bits into the open'. She continued prophetically: 'I wish I could be as sure that I'll be remembered in Aus lit[erature] as you will be: you are THERE. I may be spoken of once in a way in regard to Bark House Days . . .'.[3]

Bark House Days, the book of autobiographical sketches of her Gippsland childhood first published in 1921, is in fact the only work of Mary Fullerton's that has been reprinted in its entirety since her death. When it was brought out in 1964 by Melbourne University Press, the new foreword by Frank Dalby Davison did not focus on the book's contribution to Australian literature, as Mary would have wished, but on its value as social history. 'It would be folly to recommend *Bark House Days* as great literature', Davison decreed, seeing the book's value merely as 'an authentic fragment from Australian ways of life we shall never see again'.[4] He added that 'being a woman, she gives us much of the domestic, hearth-and-home aspect of the pioneering days'.

Miles continued to publicise Mary's poems wherever she could and the ongoing dialogue between the two women writers about poetry provided a space for them to discuss their commitments to Australian nationalism and to feminism; it also enabled them to continue to create and affirm their stance on chastity and their commitment to women's friendship. Often comparing Mary's work to that of Emily Dickinson, Miles once told her friend that Dickinson was 'acclaimed as America's greatest woman poet not only by academicians but also by the forward brigade who would canonise her if they cd only prove that she wasn't a virgin'.[5] Mary did not comment on the nineteenth-century poet's sexual status but did modestly acknowledge a resemblance to her in poetic style: 'In my less gifted way I find a touch with her which is in love of terseness and *saying the thought*, sometimes deliberately fracturing rules. An incessant smoothness in poetry cloys. Could you read Moore all day or (although splendid) Swinburne its like being drenched in nectar, one might drown while stuff like E D's makes one have to keep one's feet on the cobble stones with now and then a plunge into cool lucidity'.[6] 'I have the two Emilies deep in my heart', Mary told Miles in the same letter.

The other 'Emily' was Emily Brontë, and in 1936 the two women laughed together over a biographer's claim to have discovered a long-lost lover for the woman who had written the passionate *Wuthering Heights* but who had remained romantically unattached throughout her short life. An enthusiastic Virginia Moore had published a book on Brontë in which she read the title of a poem in handwritten manuscript as 'Louis Parensell', deducing a frustrated love affair and connecting this to what she described as the writer's 'eager death'.[7] The title was later deciphered by a reviewer of the book as 'Love's Farewell'. Mary gloated to Miles: 'Isn't the Emily Brontë fiasco a "lark"', then probed: 'They will be finding in your saga internal evidence of several heart breaking romances you've been through . . . And not even I oh most reticent know if you did ever break your heart in just that way!!'[8] Her friend did not take up the hint to confess her love life, replying, 'I am so glad about the explosion of Louis Parensell. Of course it is Love's Farewell, but you won't get the sex-besotted to believe that'.[9]

Secrets continued to be part of the currency of the friendship too, but now the identity to be protected was that of the poet, Mary Fullerton. On two occasions in early 1937 Miles gave a lecture on Mary's poetry to literary societies. Calling her lecture

'Discovery of a Poet', she grouped thematically many of the short epigrammatic poems Mary wrote in the 1930s. About the poet's identity she told Mary: 'I'll keep dark till we discuss it. You can always give out a secret but you can't pull it back'.[10]

In April 1937 the new Canberra-based literary magazine, *Australian National Review*, accepted a lengthened version of the talk for publication. The editor, W. Farmer Whyte, told Miles he had sent the article to scholar and poet, Dr L.H. Allen who, he said 'was very much struck by the article, disclosing as it does that you have discovered a *real poet*'. Whyte added, 'we are both wondering who he (or she) is! No – we do not think it is a *woman*! – but we shall be very interested to hear something further about him from you'. (Miles had typed the letter for Mary so the underlinings and exclamation marks would have been her own additions).[11]

'My Dear Miles', Mary immediately responded to Miles's success with the article, connecting her friend's interest in promoting her poetry with the quality of friendship itself: 'I'm just fair flummoxed. You are a wonder not only in perseverance but in having the spirit of perseverance over the work of another. You are rare too in another thing viz friendship. I never knew anyone else who was so disinterested. I only hope I shall never shame you. As to my feelings of gratitude I can't begin to speak of that; words fail me as the phrase has it very aptly'. Mary also said that she was 'exceedingly anxious' to remain anonymous, suggesting that '[i]f anything were pub[lished] needing signature I think G.W. for "Gippsland Woman" would do, or if you like G.G.W. which would include Glenmaggie and still keep vague'.[12]

Mary Fullerton had several good reasons for wishing to remain anonymous, one being her gender, another her age. But one of her main concerns was her lack of education, especially as she wanted to be taken seriously as a poet and felt that Australian literary criticism was becoming increasingly 'snobbish' in its 'fetish that Uni is the one and only source of imaginative lit[erature]'.[13] She wrote of her distrust of critics in 'Humility':

> The poet was exuberant,
> Along his labyrinth shouting.

'Good fellow, you must trim,'
The critics came a-clouting.

And so he cut and pruned,
At the behesting . . .
And now remain no bowers,
Nor sweet birds nesting.[14]

Miles Franklin was also sensitive and defensive about the issue of education and snobbery and developed a distrust of academic critics that engendered some vitriolic outbursts. Chief among her targets was the clique involving Marjorie Barnard, Flora Eldershaw and Frank Dalby Davison. Barnard, who had been educated at the University of Sydney, critiqued both the work of Miles Franklin and Brent of Bin Bin and, ironically, was to write the first biography of Miles after her death. Miles became increasingly sharp-tongued in later years. In 1943, for example, she told Mary that she was seeking someone to judge the book of the month for the Australian Literature Society: 'The first I asked was Margery [sic] Barnard. I thought it wd be good to exercise her bobby-dazzler critic capabilities. She is too busy lecturing this month (probably denigrating me everywhere)'.[15]

In the light of both women's sensitivities about education, we can understand that, as well as providing cover for Mary by being deliberately mysterious about the author she called 'my poet', Miles also derived great pleasure from testing both the "academics" and such established poets as Mary Gilmore. Buoyed by the publication of the *Australian National Review* article on her poet in June 1937, Miles wrote to Mary Fullerton about a meeting she attended in July as part of 'a Committee for the Sesqui centenary gift book like the one done for Melbourne'. There she met Mary Gilmore who said Miles should give some of the poems of her unknown poet, suggesting the one about the little hen's shadow, called 'Shadow'. 'I said, no', Miles told Mary, 'something great and grand, like Lion, for such a publication. Then Flora Eldershaw, who is the chairwoman, said it wd have to be a woman and I drew a long sad moan. And Barnard said, oh, well then it is a man'. Miles continues, 'My brain jumped with glee. I could not have included you because it is confined to NSW writers, but I let them think it was because of sex. Now they will think it a NSW man and that will stave off the wolves for a while and I did it all with just a deep groaning sigh. Said not a word'.[16]

Mary was delighted to receive her copy of the 'Discovery of a Poet' article in July, telling Miles that 'Mabel was excited and showed the paper to Jean (one can't stop her). I immediately swore Jean silent (she is very discreet)'. She added with fervour: 'If I could have even one line for a child to live after me I'd be content'.[17] When Miles sent her just a few weeks later a copy of a letter she had received from Mary Gilmore about the poems she had shown her, Mary once again made reference to friendship: 'All that has happened [to] these verses is due to you – to you as my friend and as a personality of great perseverance. You have the mettle of your faith so to speak, and [it is] that selflessness in your nature that is one of the rarest attributes in a friend as you have shown it to me. My past experience is of a kind of *petty jealousy* even in friends (especially if aspiring to anything in art themselves). I had one once whose jealousy would have turned me sour had my nature been one to curdle easily. Thank heavens it isn't, but it does give one an upward shove to find this very rare attribute in a friend as you have shown it to me'.[18] I wonder who the unnamed writer friend was who was jealous. It seems from the context Mary hadn't told Miles about this person before.

It was to be another five years before the first of two volumes of Mary Fullerton's poetry saw the light through the perseverance of Miles Franklin. Dedicated 'To Virginia', *Moles Do So Little With Their Privacy* was published by Angus & Robertson in 1942, Miles having enlisted the aid of poet and academic, Tom Inglis Moore. He and Miles had met every week at the Hotel Metropole where they went through the latest poems. Moore admitted later that he did not know, even though he had edited the poems, who the poet was until after Mary's death.[19]

In his preface, Moore identified the poet's gender if not her name, describing her as a poet who 'takes the universe for her continent of thought', and as 'a true symbolist' whose imagination 'sees heaven in a wildflower'. He was also critical, finding her craftsmanship 'sometimes faulty and her musical instrument limited'. Miles herself wrote an 'Explanatory Note' to the volume which, like the preface, drew attention to the poet's faults as well as her virtues, adopting a stance of objectivity that reads oddly today. I can't help wondering how Mary felt about reading that her poetry was 'wayward of form and monotonous in metre', even if her friend did praise her ability to compress 'into a quatrain a satire, a sermon, a singing lyric or a tragedy'.

The final pseudonym decided upon for *Moles* and the later volume of poetry, *The Wonder and the Apple*, was simply 'E', suggested to Mary by Miles in 1940. The choice was a secret that linked the two conspirators who shared initials, the ever-scheming Miles deciding that to use MF would be too risky: 'I wonder if we could use one of your initials. I suggest *E*, as the others are mine, and that would be a lark, but the public might think it too much of a lark as I am a suspect character in this anonymous business'.[20] It was eventually to be Miles Franklin herself who would reveal the identity of the poet 'E' – in '"E": The Full Story', her obituary article in the 'Red Page' of *The Bulletin* on 15 May 1946.

When the volume of poetry for which she had waited so long finally came out in 1942, Mary was no longer living at 181c High Street. She was staying in the relative safety of rural Sussex, waiting out the blitz that was devastating London. The writer's already poor health had deteriorated further during the years after Miles Franklin returned to Australia. Mabel was deeply concerned, writing to Miles in November 1936: 'When can you come? Your room will be ready for you. It is my room at present so that I can creep in to bed late without the anxiety of disturbing Mary. She is very fragile, constantly in some way not well. Today she has developed a cold that with others would not be serious but with her means influenza unless great care is taken. I have been bathing her feet and legs by the fire in her room, giving her a hot drink etc. That is why I started this so late. All the summer I have felt I must not leave her, even for a weekend'.[21] Mary herself adapted to her situation with her customary stoicism and quiet humour. In a letter to her sisters just before her sixty-ninth birthday in 1937, she expressed surprise that she had 'braved it so long', commenting wryly that she was '[o]ne of the creaking gate kind I suppose'.[22]

By early 1939 Mary was suffering frequently from what she referred to as 'bilious attacks'; she also had a prolonged bout of influenza after which she was confined to bed for weeks with a 'tired heart' and asthma. The threat of war was a constant worry too but, as Mary told Miles, her friend was still an activist: 'Mabel is off marching this afternoon, a girl left in charge. She is indefatigable. There is a peace march to the Park'.[23] For her part, Mary was getting ready to leave London in the event of war breaking out. This included a level of preparation which suggests that she may have feared she might not return. 'Going over old papers and letters *burning* etc' was typical of the comments in her diary at the time.[24]

The plan was for Mary to go to her married niece's farm in Sussex where she would be safer and on 2 September she noted in her diary: 'Dark day of impending War. At night great thunderstorm for hours. M[abel] listened wireless reports hourly. I go to Sophie's tomorrow'. A 'man and car' came at ten the next morning and Mabel accompanied the woman she had lived with for seventeen years to the farm near Worthing, saw her to bed and returned to London. Mary, who rarely recorded her feelings in her diary, confined her comments on this momentous shift to 'I stood journey well'. A few days later, her entry reads simply: 'Sent birthday rhyme to Mabel'.

Mabel was less reticent than her friend and confided her feelings to Miles in her letters during this difficult period, also warning her of Mary's worsening health: 'You must accept the fact of Mary being an invalid Miles, dear, a beautiful soul coming to the end of a long, wonderful and oft times tiresome journey. I should be ashamed to let my personal grief mar in any way what is perhaps the most peaceful period of our friendship. . . . She is coming to the parting of the ways. We talk of it quite calmly'. She finishes this long letter, written at 11pm, with 'It is strange here without her . . . I do not like going into her empty room – and the future? I wonder – but what's the use'.[25]

The gregarious Mabel Singleton was now alone at the Kensington flat. Denis had married Eileen Reid in 1935 and they lived with their young daughter, Valerie, at Hitchin in Hertfordshire where Denis was stationed with the Air Force. Jean Hamilton still worked in the office but relations between the two women had reached a new low point after Jean took up an interest in religion. Mabel confided to Miles in the letter written just after Mary's departure: 'Jean taxes me to the utmost. We are about as diametrically opposed in our outlook and in our attitude to world affairs as two people could be . . . She is so smug, so self-satisfied, it is dreadful'.[26] Jean's own letters to Miles during the war seem to give Mabel's criticisms some validity. In one she complains about people running back and forth to shelters to avoid the bombing, commenting self-righteously: 'It is interesting to observe how little religion has helped nervous minds. It is the spiritual test for all those who accept a God . . . I sleep under my glass roof in peace always'.[27] Even Mary complained to Miles in 1941 that 'Jean keeps well but is a sore trial with her preachings to all who come . . . It is a pity people take up with such bunkum religions'.[28]

The situation at Worthing was difficult for Mary as her niece and her husband were, in Mabel's words, 'ardent followers' of Oswald Mosley, who formed the British Union of Fascists.[29] Three weeks after leaving London she moved again, ten miles further on to Sandbank, the home of a musician, Beatrice Williams, whose live-in companion was Mrs Reid, Eileen's mother. Mary wrote to Miles of her new situation in November: 'Miss Williams is a musical lady, has a fine violin bought in Italy long ago for 250 pounds. She has been running an orchestra in Brighton for years. Now all this is suspended . . . She is very kind indeed to me I don't know why just her nature I suppose. Anyhow I feel grateful to be made so much at home and looked after so well. Eileen's mother too is good to me. Fact is I pay 15/– a week bare and quite inadequate but all I can afford, it is fortunate I hadn't blued up my little savings'.[30] Sandbank, between the tiny village of Maresfield and the small town of Uckfield, was to be Mary's home for the rest of her life.

In spite of being confined mostly to bed and separated from

Mabel, except for her weekly visit, Mary remained in good spirits, writing letters and poems and starting work on her memoirs. Her diary notes that she lent her typewriter for war work just after arriving at Sandbank and her manuscripts and letters are from then on handwritten, except for her memoirs, which Miles and Mabel paid to have typed. Miles asked Mabel in early 1940 if Mary was in any discomfort, commenting that '[b]y her letters there would seem to be an exhilaration of tragedy which sustains her – keeps her from inanition'.[31] Certainly the stoicism for which she was renowned is apparent in many of Mary's diary entries. Although safer than London, the situation in Sussex was still constantly tense and the entry for 27 August 1940 read: 'Raids. Sirens nearly all night. Others went to Shelter. I stayed house, asthma. Wrote Miles, sent various verses'.

Mabel's attempt to reassure Miles about Mary's comfort also reveals some tensions in the household at Sandbank and, as usual, Mabel (who Mary once confessed was so outspoken that it sometimes made her hair 'stand with surprise') does not hold back on the gossip: 'I wish you could see her – such a picture of comfort, with the low window near the foot of the bed. Miss Williams is so wise in all she does for Mary, sends the curtain that would shut out the view 'wizzing' to the other side of the window: the sort of things you and I would do to make her restful and happy. Mrs Read [sic] is more prim and with all her goodness inclined to be petty and irritate M[ary] who has the wisdom to turn the pin-pricking to jokes! She keeps them amused: writing amusing verses about their friends and any incident that calls forth her unfailing sense of humour. They love her and through her like each other better. What a blessing it is that she can be there'.[32]

It seems Mary may have used her sense of humour not only to make the atmosphere more congenial at Sandbank but as a strategy of self-preservation, turning her annoyance into gentle satire in her letters. She told her sisters a long story about the dog swallowing a box of matches, after which Miss Williams and Mrs Reid chased him around the house with castor oil: 'The dog has a mania for matches. He must be ready for spontaneous combustion like Dickens' old man Krank or some such name.

English ladies sure are crazy over dogs – and bishops'.[33] In 1941 she wrote to Miles of Mrs Reid's grandmotherly zeal over the expected birth of Denis and Eileen's second child: 'Mrs R has knitted little swalloping and swaddling and twiddling and twaddling garments for weeks past and is now going furiously at a bed jacket for Eileen this very handsome in pale pastel shades of blue and pink. Don't you wish you were having a baby to have such a tog?'.[34] Mary stressed the importance of retaining her sense of humour in the memoirs she wrote while she was in Sussex: 'I'd have gone down, I think, under the pressure of personal ills, added to the natural melancholy of my outlook, but for this capacity to see the humorous element that runs like a streak of lightning through the grey fabric of life. (I mix my metaphors)'.[35]

When the flat at 181c High Street suffered damage in a bombing raid in 1940, Mabel wrote up the event in the style of a short story, getting it typed up by a friend. She sent it to Mary's sisters, informing them that Mary herself was not to be told. In it she describes the event in vivid detail: 'About 7.45 pm on 7th October, 1940, a bomb was dropped on the small Cinema behind No 181c, High Street, Kensington, W8. I had just finished a meal in the top back room (kitchen - dining-room), and went on to the landing as soon as the siren sounded. A few seconds later the ceiling fell down, the windows were blown in with the frames, and in the lavatory and bathroom next to it also, and water poured down from the roof tank like a waterfall, doing most damage to the floor below, and still more to the Lawyer's premises below the two floors of 181c'. She also tells how she goes every night since the bombing to a shelter which holds 400 people, six minutes walk away 'in Pontings' new building': 'There are a lot of two tier bunks, and many sleep on the floor – one is as hard as the other! No-one undresses. It is a most amazing sight, you can imagine. Most of us bring our suppers, as the Siren goes early most nights, and also people like to come as soon after dark as they can. What an existence!! I read the papers, write letters, play with children, talk a little (not more than is necessary to be agreeable). I like to get up on my bunk and survey the scene – and wonder and wonder and wonder . . . !'[36]

Mabel probably sent a copy of the story to Miles too who

wrote to Mary in December saying: 'I have just had a letter from Mabel giving me details of her shelter under the store. I am glad it is so comfortable and that she can get a bit of sleep to carry on the days. She is wonderful. I wish I were under her wing too; zest might return to my life'.[37] It seems Mary remained unaware of the bombing, simply recording in her diary: 'M[abel] came 4.30. Now sleeping at night in Shelter near St Mary Abbots. I'm glad. Safer than flat. Weekend away from London helps her.'[38]

The stresses of running the business, enduring the bombing raids, going to the shelter at night, as well as travelling to Sussex to see Mary on the weekends and watching her illness progress, all took their toll on Mabel's nerves and physical health. Gradually she let Jean take over the business and spent more time at Sandbank, sharing Mary's room and looking after her. Jean was quite happy with the arrangement as she told Miles: 'Virginia has been away in the country coming up to London once in two or three weeks for a day and sometimes two if quiet. She has been in a very highly nervous condition mentally and physically since the war and it's a relief to think of her gaining a little ground by being with Mary in the country . . . Fear is the most dominant and shattering vibration in any conditions so I'm deeply grateful to have the lady in the country'.[39] Mabel herself acknowledged to Miles that the arrangement suited them both: 'Jean said she had heard from you when I was last at 181c. I am very grateful to her for carrying on alone: she is much happier doing so than working with me, and financially much better off: rightly so'.[40]

Among the poems Mary wrote during the years she spent in Sussex are several that were written with dedications to Mabel. One called 'Pattern', handwritten in ink on blue paper and dated 11 November 1941, speaks eloquently of their life together:

> The subtle beauty of the joys that came
> And shed a light on us, so near, so clear
> So that we realized the light
> Was not the prism of a tear.
> The subtle beauty of the griefs gone by,
> That left a silver veil on you and me
> Prickt with the taper-points of joy –
> The pattern of mortality.

It seems as though the two women were still able to take pleasure in their relationship even though Mary was so ill by 1944 that Mabel told Miles she was taking 'medicine with morphia in it; as many as 5 doses in 24 hrs'. In the same letter, she recounts: 'Mary and I had an amusing "bout" one day when she said it would have been interesting to have had different parents: too literally (as usual) I replied that there would be no "Mary and Mabel" had we not had our own parents!! and we both talked a lot of nonsense!! Yesterday we had a very amusing talk about the *devil* without laying claim to being original we agreed in the end that we felt sorry for him!'.[41]

In September 1944 Denis and Eileen made a rare visit to Sussex for two days, mainly to see Mary. Both were 'looking tired and on the thin side'. Denis was in charge of the Air Force base at Hitchin, for which he was awarded an OBE in 1945; Eileen was looking after their two children as well as doing underground work at 'Bomber Command'. To Miles, Mary confided that she was in her 'best form . . . So they saw my thinness but otherwise avoided being shocked. Their goodbye privately affected me so wistful yet striving to be casual. I *may* see them again, who knows'.[42]

Miles continued to write long letters to Mary full of literary gossip; she also finished nearly all of them with words of praise for Mabel and for their friendship. 'Mabel is a glorious nurse. Her hands give such comfort. They have strength as well as kindness in them – not like the little claws of you and me', she wrote in March 1945. A month later: 'Mary, my dear, how wonderful it is to have a friend like Mabel, so dear and good and capable. If only we each could be seen off by someone like that'.[43] To Mabel she wrote: 'Mary has a strong fragility or a fragile strength that is miraculous, and of course your great friendship is oil to both lamps'.[44]

Mary was too ill to be moved back to London when the war ended in 1945 and Beatrice Williams suggested both Mary and Mabel stay on at Sandbank. In early January 1946 Mabel told Miles: 'Mary is so ill the Dr thinks she cannot recover as she has so many times. And Miles no-one could wish her to live on to suffer as she does now, constantly'.[45] She rallied again, but at the end of the month Mabel wrote: 'Her life is complete Miles, and what a life, what an example. I know of no-one who has come into contact with her who has not loved her. Denis has always divided his love of parents between us and I have been happy in the knowledge of this, and of her devotion to him; quite unique in human experience I believe'.[46]

On 8 February she wrote: 'Mary is very near the close of her life . . . My love for her is greater than for anyone else in the world and I shall need all my courage, and much else to face up to life without her'. She finished the letter: 'I seem to know her thoughts and often anticipate them. "How did you know I wanted you to do that" Mary would ask. We have always joked; in responding to her humour mine has developed. Mary is sleeping now, but wld send deep love and affection with mine. Yours ever, Mabel'.

Mary Fullerton died peacefully at 3 a.m. on 23 February 1946. On the day of her funeral, at which Mary's cousin Victor officiated in the Maresfield church, Miles pictured the scene in a letter to Emily Fullerton: 'It will be cold and perhaps grey but the little cool spring flowers that she so much loved will be well on the way. Mary could have described the scene exquisitely in one of her philosophical lyrics'.[47] One such poem in *The Wonder and the Apple*, the volume of Mary Fullerton's poetry published just after her death, appears to sum up the philosophy of this reticent writer, whose 'violet's eye' perspective on life was her strength:

> 'Withdrawn'
>
> The butterflies are never still,
> Thin bird legs dance upon my sill;
> Great patronizing hollyhocks
> Nod to the flaunting crimson phlox;
> Borders of gentian cry "Behold,
> This is a world of blue and gold."
> The rose sits on her latticed throne,
>
> Five pigeons burnish on the stone;
> The peacock brawls along the lawn,
> The sunflower's phalanxes are drawn.
>   . . .
> In a green nook the violet's eye
> In beauty and sobriety,
> Cons, past the moment's glow and strife,
> The quiet biography of life.[48]

171

POSTSCRIPT

Almost immediately after Mary's death, Mabel left for Walsall to visit her step sister who was seriously ill and who 'took her life' shortly afterwards.[1] She returned a few days later via 181c High Street to Sandbank 'to finish the clearing up'. After explaining her movements to Miles, she wrote: 'It is well one has to carry on when the feeling that everything must stand still for a time possesses one; that it is necessary to write commonplace explanations like the above, when one's heart is full of tears and loneliness and the "carrying on" requires an almost superhuman effort'.[2] Even after the loss of her friend, Mabel's energy and practicality is what sustained her.

In Sydney, Miles Franklin tried to publicise the volume of 'E's' poetry that was brought out by Angus & Robertson just after Mary's death, partly through keeping alive the mystery of the poet's identity. On 23 March 1946, however, an article written by A.H. Chisholm from Angus & Robertson appeared in the *Melbourne Herald*, headed 'Two Noted Women Writers Die', which revealed that 'E' was Mary Fullerton. Miles was pleased with the opening of the article: 'Two of Australia's most distinguished women writers, Henry Handel Richardson and Mary Fullerton, both of whom lived abroad for many years, died in England within a few weeks of each other'. But she was horrified by the revelation of the secret and by the author's condescending description of Mary's poetry: 'I hope you note the studied insult twice they mention *verse* but not *poetry*', she wrote to Emily Fullerton. '*E* was a poet. *Mary* is a mere *versifier*. I know the member of the clique that came from, one whom Mary feared in the literary way and who is now taking care that once the anonymity is to be exploded that Mary is put back in her place as a *versifier. Competent verse!!!*'[3]

Miles Franklin's response to the revelation was to publish a glowing obituary in the Red Page of *The Bulletin* on 15 May, under the title, '"E": The Full Story'. In it, she describes Mary Fullerton as 'sensitive, fastidious, reticent, self-mastered' with a 'spiritual tenacity' that 'remained inviolable'; her poetic talent she describes as an 'exquisite gift'. She couldn't resist a dig at academia, referring to '[a]n uninspired professor of literature' who 'had doubted if there were one successful line in her first collections', a judgement she said her friend knew came from the academic's knowledge that 'she had never even seen the doormat of a university'. The article does not leave out Mabel Singleton: Miles praises her for her devotion to her friend, especially in the last years when Mary was so ill, managing as well to tie this in to a plug for E's earlier volume of poetry by revealing another secret: '"My dear beautiful friend, Mabel," as Mary said so often near the end, and this is the Virginia of the dedication to *Moles*'.

In spite of her efforts, *The Wonder and the Apple* continued to sell very slowly, Miles telling Emily that '[a]ll they cared about the poet E was to find out who she was and now they have no further interest'.[4] Emily was not surprised at the book's failure to sell, commenting to Miles, 'I'm not one atom surprised. I can't think of one person I know whose taste it would be. To me it's like trying to read Mabel's and Miss Williamson's[sic] letters – about as understandable'. She continues: 'Mary would rather I said what I thought than pretended to like it when I don't. No doubt the few that sold at first were to literary people who like things to puzzle over, and gammon they understand. Poor Mary. A pity her writings were mostly so involved. It's no use Mabel gammoning she has the hang of them all. I don't believe her'.[5] (Miles has written at the top of this letter: 'Mary's family had no understanding of her talent, only of her lack of success'.) Towards the end of 1948, when it was clear sales had dried up, Miles asked Emily how many copies of the book she would like, adding 'I'll get some for myself and some to send to Mabel. It wd be nice to keep some on hand and send others instead of Christmas cards to everyone interested. They say I can have as many as I like free of charge. I wonder how many I dare ask for'.[6]

Mabel Singleton herself had little money in her later years. She sold the business in 1948 but, according to Jean Hamilton, 'made a deal with difficult people'.[7] Mabel told Miles that Jean had taken the profits and paid no taxes. As she was preparing to pack up and leave 181c in the May of '48, Mabel wrote to Miles: 'So will end a long strange chapter in my life, much happiness in the earlier years; great unhappiness during the last years'.[8] The relationship between Mabel and Jean was then completely severed and Jean started her own agency not far from the Kensington office. The correspondence between Jean and Miles continued fitfully, Jean's handwritten air letters becoming almost impossible to decipher. She died of cancer in 1961.

After the sale of the business Mabel, who had spent so many years running her own domestic hiring agency, took up a series of live-in domestic posts herself, among them cooking in a vegetarian guesthouse, looking after a child, and care-taking a cousin's house. Miles wrote to her in 1949, saying, 'Will you always have to keep on and on? Won't there be a time when you can be at peace even in a tiny flatette or one room and go through your papers and write up your memoirs of Mary – just for your own pleasure and to leave the MSS to the Mitchell if it is not wanted by publishers'.[9]

Miles had been urging Mabel to write about her friendship with Mary from her first letter after her friend's death. She gave detailed advice as to how to go about it: 'Get exercise books – they are the best as separate leaves get astray. Write one side of page only with plenty of margin, put things down just as they come to your heart and memory – just as they come – they can be set in proper chronology later. A first draft contains much that can be rearranged or dropped. This will be a big and important and wonderful thing. It is your responsibility, and will be your reward, I know'.[10] Later, when Mabel was still procrastinating, she suggested: 'The way to get your story would be just to talk it out and then perhaps I could suggest about the form and sequence of events. You would need a dictaphone . . . Dymphna Cusack is a business-like person like you, and typing drives her nervous, so she got a dictaphone lately and says it is saving her years of time and wear and tear . . . If you really think of doing a story – and it wd be an adventure to keep us from moping on the shelf – why not make enquiries about getting a dictaphone'.[11]

Mabel talked frequently about trying to get out to Australia so that she and Miles could work on the story together. 'If I were younger I wld work my passage out, but at 70 it is not easy', she wrote to Miles at the end of 1946.[12] She did not make it to Australia, nor did she write about her life with Mary, but in 1952 Mabel told her friend in Australia: 'You will always belong intimately with the friendship between Mary and me, a part of it, and nothing can change that'.[13]

The correspondence between the two women became increasingly sad as the years passed and friends and colleagues died. In 1950, Mabel had written to Miles that she'd had a letter from Nettie Palmer telling her they were planning to create a scholarship in modern history to commemorate the memory of Vida Goldstein. Mabel had not heard of her death but said she told Nettie, who 'thought I could unearth old friends over here who might be interested', that 'she had forgotten how long ago it is: more than 30 years since we came to live in England again and even then Vida had given up the political work Mary and I helped in and was interested only in C[hristian] Science'.[14] Miles replied: 'Yes, there is no one left hardly to remember Vida Goldstein and she retired into Christian Science which was equivalent to entering a nunnery to take her out of the public eye. People are soon forgotten, someone the other day came to ask me who was Rose Scott'.[15]

Miles Franklin herself died four years after this letter, in 1954, just before what would have been her seventy-fifth birthday. In accordance with her wishes, her ashes were scattered over Jounama Creek at her birthplace, Talbingo. Mabel Singleton lived till the age of eighty-eight, spending the last period of her life in a nursing home in Hertfordshire. She died on 30 December 1965.

What Mabel Singleton's version of the story of her friendship with Mary Fullerton would have contained will remain a mystery. There are so many ways of telling that story. Emily Fullerton gave her summary of it to John Moir in 1952 when he was setting up the La Trobe collection of Australiana at the State Library of Victoria. He had acquired, at Miles Franklin's instigation, the letters and papers Mabel had sent to Arden after Mary's death. 'Dear Mr

Moir', Mary's sister wrote, 'I'll drop a line at once and answer your questions. Mabel is Mary's very dear friend (also Miles's) Mrs Singleton. Mary lived with her in Kensington London all the years until the bombing began then she lived and died at Miss Williams in Sussex. Miles stayed a year in Kensington with them when she returned from America – Mabel had a registery office in High St Kensington but she neglected it very much the last year to nurse Mary. Denis is Mabel's son (born out here) and was in charge of a drome north of England during the war. Eileen is his wife – Valerie, Michael their children. I hear from Mrs Singleton fairly often – she has never got over Mary's death'.[16] Many of the elements of the story told in these pages are present in this account, but the emphasis is different as was the sisters' understanding of Mary and Mabel's relationship.

My version of the friendship between Mary Fullerton, Mabel Singleton and Miles Franklin is completed, but there are many unanswered questions that must remain tantalisingly suspended. We can glean a sense of Mary's passion for her 'beloved immediate friend,/The chosen of my heart' from the poems she wrote to Mabel. But how did Mabel herself perceive the relationship? I suspect we would not have been given any intimate insights even if she *had* written her memoir for 'the world at large'.[17] What could be told publicly was one of the sticking points she related to Miles. And why was Miles Franklin so insistent that Mabel write the story of the friendship? One reason was certainly that such a story might lift the sales of *The Wonder and the Apple*, which sold little more than one hundred copies. She also wanted to protect the friendship from what the 'newshounds' might make of it 'when we are gone', as she told Mabel, indicating that she was aware it could be construed as a lesbian relationship?[18] But could there also have been a desire on Miles's part to know more about what made this friendship work, even to understand what she might have not allowed herself in her relationships with women?

The tendency to depict historical "passionate friendships" between women as unfailingly warm and tender romanticises and idealises them; at worst, such a depiction is trivialising and condescending. The material I have retrieved from library archives about the women whose lives are represented in these pages shows that such friendships as the one between Mary Fullerton and Mabel Singleton shared all the intricate emotional dynamics of relationships between women and men. This relationship also evolved and changed over the years, requiring negotiations and compromises in order to survive. Passionate friendships had particular problems too, relating to their unsanctioned nature, problems that still exist for women in lesbian relationships today, even though they may manifest themselves differently. Such friendships did not exist in isolation either, but needed the support of other women. The volatility of the friendship network at 181c High Street shows just how complicated such networks could become. These also change and evolve. The friendship between Mary Fullerton and Miles Franklin started because of their shared interest in writing and their expatriate Australian status. Over the years it developed and changed, eventually taking on a third dimension as Mabel Singleton and Miles Franklin gained support from each other during Mary's illness and subsequent death.

Making meaning of the past is something that we invent in the present; it can never be the "true story" of what happened. But the exploration can help us understand how meaning is made according to what knowledges are available, what is 'in the air' at any particular time and place. I have found women's friendships to be complex creations with fluid boundaries; they can serve diverse purposes and satisfy a range of desires, including sexual desire. I believe Mary Fullerton was neither what we would call today a closeted lesbian nor a woman who was unaware of her predilection for her own sex.

Many marginalised groups find the current "postmodern" climate that resists certainties and absolutes understandably threatening to their hard-fought negotiations of identity. Yet I think it is possible to shift the emphasis from what is "true" to what is at stake in our differing stories. Out of the present climate the notion of a queer perspective has emerged, a diverse concept that is less a new identity than a critique of identity, or at least of the politics of identity. Like Mary Fullerton at the beginning of this century, some women today do not refer to their same-sex desires as "lesbian". They eschew the term for different reasons from those I have suggested for Mary, but also because they, like her, do not wish to be constrained by the boundaries of that term. If, however, such identities as lesbian can be understood queerly as shifting and unfixable, then I believe they have not yet reached their "use-by" date.

Exploring the past not only allows us to understand our present better by calling into question understandings that many of us take for granted as fixed, it can also help us to "become" rather than, in the terms of the late twentieth century, to "come out". It is a process I find constantly fascinating, in spite of the difficulties those of us who don't conform to conventional life patterns face. Mary Fullerton struggled in her poetry to find a language to articulate her desire for Mabel Singleton; I have tried to suggest my own readings of these poems. But Mary also knew that such desires remain elusive and the expression of them ultimately mysterious. In 1941 she wrote 'Imponderable', which begins:

> Feeling can have no framed
> Solidity,
> Nor love a stable shape
> Nor can you measure me.

On a cold December day my partner Lizzie and I searched the deserted, overgrown cemetery in the grounds of St Bartholomew's Church at Maresfield for signs of Mary Fullerton's grave. It was a silent world. Soft rain drifted down from a grey-blanketed sky and our boots made no sound as we moved through the long wet grass that gradually saturated the bottoms of our jeans. There were many Marys and nearly as many Elizas, but we could find no Mary Eliza Fullerton on the faded headstones. Disappointed, we walked the few kilometres back to Uckfield – the end of the line for British Rail – and caught the train back to London, retracing the journey Mabel Singleton made so often in the early

1940s. At least we did not have to worry about the possibility of 'air activity' that concerned Mary when her friend travelled.

Denis Singleton later told me that he understands there is a headstone, in the lower part of the graveyard furthest from the road. It must have been put there after 1952, when Mabel said to Miles that she wondered why Mary's relations had not 'paid for a small cross or something quite simple for her grave'.[19] So, although I was disappointed in my desire to find a visible marker to neatly conclude the search for Mary Fullerton that had taken up several years of my life, I can't help feeling that she has somehow had the last word by insisting on remaining hidden, thereby retaining her violet's eye view of the world.

ABBREVIATIONS

AG	Aileen Goldstein
AGR	Alice Grant Rosman
EF	Emily Fullerton
FL	Fawcett Library, City of London Polytechnic
FP	Franklin Papers
JH	Jean Hamilton
MDR	Mary Dreier Robins
MEF	Mary Eliza Fullerton
MES	Mabel Ethel Singleton
ML	Mitchell Library
NLA	National Library of Australia
SMF	Stella Miles Franklin
SLV	State Library of Victoria (La Trobe Collection)
VG	Vida Goldstein
WS	Winifred Stephensen
WV	*Woman Voter*

PROLOGUE

1. In MEF to SMF, n.d. (but probably 1934), FP16.
2. Mary Fullerton Papers, ML 2342/10.

CHAPTER 1
THE WOMEN BEHIND THE WORDS

1. SMF to MEF, 3/8/30, FP16.
2. Fullerton papers, ML 2342/10. All quotations from Mary Fullerton's poetry will be taken from this source unless otherwise stated.
3. W.H. Wilde and T. Inglis Moore (eds), *Letters of Mary Gilmore*, p.135.
4. *Moles*, Preface, p.7; p.52.
5. *The Breaking Furrow*, p.52.
6. Examples are the entries in the *Australian Dictionary of Biography* and Heather Radi (ed), *200 Australian Women.*
7. Colin Roderick, *Miles Franklin: Her Brilliant Career.*
8. Drusilla Modjeska, *Exiles at Home*, p.156.
9. See, for example, Jill Roe, *My Congenials*; Verna Coleman, *Miles Franklin in America.*
10. Lillian Faderman, *Surpassing The Love of Men*; Carroll Smith-Rosenberg, 'The Female World of Love and Ritual'.
11. Graham Little, interviewed on ABC Radio's *Life Matters*, 18/11/93.
12. Eve Kosofsky Sedgewick, *The Epistemology of the Closet.*
13. Memoirs, Fullerton Papers, ML 2342/2, p.59–60.
14. Daphne Marlatt, 'Self-representation and fictionalysis'.
15. MEF to SMF, 23/10/29, FP16.

16. MES to SMF, 24/4/46, 26/8/46, 24/2/53, FP25.

CHAPTER 2
MARY

1. Memoirs, p.143.
2. Ibid., p.186.
3. Ibid., p.143.
4. MEF to SMF, 30/6/30, FP16.
5. Memoirs, p.74.
6. *Bark House Days*, p.103.
7. Ibid., p.19.
8. The Guide to the Mary Fullerton Papers and all subsequent biographical mentions of Mary Fullerton list her birth date as 14 May 1868. From internal evidence from the papers and letters, including her 1922 passport, 14 April is the correct date.
9. Ibid., p.11.
10. Don Watson, *Caledonia Australis*, p.xviii. I am indebted to this fine revisionist history of Gippsland for the details of the region's settlement.
11. *Bark House Days*, p.39.
12. Ibid., p.20.
13. Ibid., p.25.
14. Ibid., p.24.
15. Memoirs, p.15.
16. *Bark House Days*, p.178.
17. Memoirs, p.125.
18. MEF to SMF, 31/7/28, FP16.
19. Ibid.
20. *Clare* in *Two Women*, pp.14–15.
21. Memoirs, p.61.
22. MEF to SMF, 22/7/34, FP16.
23. *Bark House Days*, p.138.
24. Ibid., p.164.
25. Ibid., p.186.
26. Memoirs, p.147.
27. Moir Papers, SLV Box 77/2.
28. Ibid., Box 77/3.
29. Ibid., Box 77/2.

CHAPTER 3
MABEL AND MILES

1. Memoirs, p.140.
2. MES to SMF, 11/12/38, FP25.
3. This information comes from an article in *Table Talk*, 9 May 1935: 'A Pioneer's Home Passes'. There are many factual inaccuracies in this article and I have not been able to verify this story.
4. Goldstein Papers, FL.
5. Miles *Franklin: A Tribute*, p.37.
6. Letter to J.B. Pinker, cited in Elizabeth Webby's Introduction to *My Brilliant Career*, 1990, p.vii.
7. Cited in Judith A. Allen, *Rose Scott*, p.141.
8. Miles Franklin, 'Rose Scott', p.102.
9. Ibid., p.100.
10. SMF to AG, 22/6/47, FP10.
11. *Women's Sphere*, 15 April, 1904.
12. VG to SMF, 26/5/04, FP10.
13. AG to SMF, 24/5/04, FP10.
14. Cited in Diane Kirkby, *Alice Henry*, p.88.
15. Ibid., pp.92–3.
16. Cited in Jill Roe, V.1, p.97.
17. SMF to MEF, 13/2/29, FP119.
18. Carolyn Heilbrun, *Writing a Woman's Life*, p.108.

CHAPTER 4
SUFFRAGISTS AND PACIFISTS

1. Farley Kelly, 'The "Woman Question" in Melbourne 1880–1914', Ch.9.
2. *WV*, December 1909.
3. Ibid., 5 July 1917.
4. Lis Whitelaw, *The Life and Rebellious Times of Cicely Hamilton*, p.60.
5. *WV*, July 1910.
6. Ibid., September 1910.

7. MEF to SMF, 26/3/29, FP16.
8. *WV*, 31 May 1917.
9. Neville Hicks, *This Sin and Scandal*, p.120.
10. *WV*, 5 May 1914.
11. Published in both *Fellowship* and *Ross's Monthly*.
12. *WV*, 1 July 1913.
13. Fullerton Papers, NLA.
14. *WV*, 10 June 1912, 11 July 1912.
15. Ibid., 26 August 1913.
16. Ibid., 21 February 1918.
17. Janette M. Bomford, *That Dangerous and Persuasive Woman: Vida Goldstein*, p.129.
18. Ibid., p.135.
19. *WV*, 10 November 1914.
20. Ibid., 1 June 1916.
21. Ibid., 21 November 1918.
22. Ibid., 26 October 1916.
23. Bomford, p.172.
24. Farley Kelly, 'Vida Goldstein: Political Woman' in M. Lake and F. Kelly, eds., *Double Time*, p.177.
25. Ibid., p.176; Bomford, p.220.
26. Kelly, p.177.
27. MEF to SMF, 4/6/29, FP16.
28. Bomford, P.200.
29. MEF to sisters, 26/1/26, NLA.
30. Ibid., 27/12/29.
31. Bomford., pp.176, 186, 162.
32. MEF to sisters, 23/7/24, Moir Papers, SLV Box 78/1a.
33. Pat Gowland, 'The Women's Peace Army' in E. Windschuttle, ed., *Women, Class and History*, pp.229–30.
34. Adrienne Rich, 'Compulsory Heterosexuality and Lesbian Existence.
35. Lillian Faderman, *Surpassing the Love of Men*, p.248.
36. Teresa de Lauretis, *The Practice of Love*, p.116.
37. Moir Papers, SLV Box 77/3.

CHAPTER 5
POETRY AND DESIRE

1. *WV*, 29 June 1916.
2. MEF to SMF, 18/11/29, FP16.
3. Memoirs, p.146.
4. Ibid., p.76.
5. Ralph Waldo Emerson, *Essays*, p.45.
6. Ibid., p.48.
7. de Lauretis, p.284.
8. *Moles Do So Little With Their Privacy*, p.34.
9. *The Wonder and the Apple*, p.32.
10. Moir Papers, SLV Box 77/1.

CHAPTER 6
A CHILD IS BORN

1. *WV*, 6 March 1911.
2. Ibid., 6 April 1911.
3. MES to EF, 22/10/45, FP121.
4. MEF to SMF, 14/1/29, FP16.
5. *WV*, 6 April 1911.
6. MEF to MP, 18/9/11, Pitt Papers, SLV 20/3c.
7. *Table Talk*, 9 May 1935.

CHAPTER 7
TO ENGLAND AND BACK

1. MEF to sisters, n.d., NLA.
2. Liz Stanley and Ann Morley, *The Life and Death of Emily Wilding Davison*, p.72.
3. *WV*, 4 November 1913.
4. Ibid, 9 December 1913.
5. AGR to MEF, 7/8/13, Moir Papers, SLV Box 78/6.
6. Ibid., 30/6/13.
7. MEF to SMF, 14/1/29, FP16.

CHAPTER 8
'I TO THE GUARD BELONG'

1. 'Memoirs', p.70.
2. Noel Greig, ed., *Edward Carpenter: Selected Writings*, Vol.1, p.9.
3. Edward Carpenter, *The Intermediate Sex*, pp.35–6.

4. Frank Bongiorno, 'Love and Friendship: Ethical Socialism in Britain and Australia', *Australian Historical Studies*, April 2001.

5. *Socialist*, 30 May 1919, p.3. I am grateful to Frank Bongiorno for directing me to this reference.

6. Greig, p.11.

7. Edward Carpenter, *Towards Democracy*, p.394.

8. MEF to SMF, 23/10/29,FP16.

9. Carpenter, *The Intermediate Sex*, p.116.

10. See Liz Stanley, 'Romantic Friendship? Some Issues in researching Lesbian History and Biography' for a discussion of some of these correspondents.

11. Cited in Bongiorno, p.9.

12. This letter by Kathlyn Oliver is published in full (under a pseudonym) in Ruth F. Claus, 'Confronting Homosexuality'.

13. Tierl Thompson, ed., *Dear Girl*, p.211.

14. Carpenter, *The Intermediate Sex*, p.199.

15. MEF to sisters, 9/3/23, NLA.

16. *Two Women: Clare: Margaret*, p.58.

17. MEF to SMF, 7/12/33, FP16.

18. *Two Women*, p.161.

19. Cited in June Rose, *Marie Stopes and the Sexual Revolution*, p.116.

20. *The Nation & The Athenaeum*, 8 December 1923, p.396.

21. C.A. Dawson Scott, *The Bookman*, 23 December 1923.

CHAPTER 9
ENGLAND: NEW BEGINNINGS

1. MEF to sisters, 28/2/22, NLA.

2. MES to Arden, 15/6/22, NLA.

3. Ibid.

4. Bomford, p.13.

5. MES to Arden, 15/6/22, NLA.

6. MEF to sisters, 23/7/24, Moir Papers, SLV Box 78/1a.

7. MES to SMF, 4/12/52, FP25.

8. MES to SMF, 24/2/53, FP25.

9. Lyd to sisters, 10/6/25, NLA.

10. MEF to sisters, June 1924, NLA.

11. MEF to EF, 3/7/23, NLA.

12. Ibid.

13. MEF to sisters, March 1925, NLA.

14. MEF to SMF, 11/1/28, FP16.

15. Ibid.

16. MEF to SMF, 31/7/28, FP16.

17. MEF to SMF, 29/10/28, FP16.

18. MEF to sisters, 11/11/29, NLA.

19. MEF to sisters, 27/12/29, NLA.

20. SMF to MEF, 18/2/[30], FP120.

21. MEF to SMF, 8/10/30, FP16.

22. MEF to SMF, 29/10/30, FP16.

23. MES to Arden, 15/6/22, NLA.

24. MEF to sisters, 15/5/28, NLA.

25. MEF to SMF, 25/2/29, FP16.

26. Cited in Modjeska, *Exiles at Home*, p.97.

27. MEF to SMF, 23/4/29, FP16.

CHAPTER 10
MEETING MILES

1. MEF to SMF, 11/4/41, FP18.

2. Cited in Roe, *My Congenials*, Vol. 1, p.120.

3. Cecil and Celia Manson, *Doctor Agnes Bennett*, p.25.

4. Cited in Roe, *My Congenials*, Vol.1, p.121.

5. Verna Coleman, *Miles Franklin in America*, p.84.

6. Cited in Roe, *My Congenials*, Vol.1, p.60.

7. Cited in Roe, *My Congenials*, Vol.1, p.97.

8. See Jill Roe, *The Significant Silence: Miles Franklin's Middle Years*.

9 . Cited in Roe, *My Congenials*, Vol.1, p. 169.

10. ABC Radio, *The Coming Out Show*, 18 August 1979.

11. Cited in Roe, *My Congenials*, Vol.1, p.171–72.

12. Diary, 7/1/27, FP2.

13. SMF to MEF, 10/6/24, NLA.

14. Diary, 19/7/26, FP2.

15. Ibid., 18/1/27.

16. Ibid., 24/3/27.

17. SMF to MEF, 14/8/[27], FP120.

18. Notebook, 1935–52, FP MSS1360, pp.14, 94, 57.

19. Barnard, ABC Radio, *The Coming Out Show*, 18 August 1979.

CHAPTER 11

THE CHASTITY KNOT

1 . MEF to SMF, 23/4/29, FP16.

2 . SMF to MEF, 17/6/29, FP16.

3 . Letter by Alice Wilson, *Australian Woman's Sphere*, 10 June 1903.

4 . *My Career Goes Bung*, p.300.

5 . MEF to SMF, 'Tailend of June' 1930, FP16.

6 . See Vera Brittain, *Radclyffe Hall: A Case of Obscenity?*.

7 . MEF to SMF, 30/7/29, FP16.

8 . Andrew Parker et al, eds., *Nationalisms and Sexualities*, p.2.

9 . Ibid.p.6.

10. MEF to SMF, 27/3/28, FP16.

11. MEF to SMF, 25/3/29, FP16.

12. Notebooks, V.1, FP3.

13. MEF to SMF, 6/5/30, FP16.

14. MEF to SMF, 28/9/36, FP16.

15. MEF to SMF, 18/8/37, FP17.

16. Barbara Holloway, 'Woman in Federation Poetry' in Susan Magarey et al, eds, *Debutante Nation*, p.160.

17. *Bark House Days*, p.42.

18. Cited in Roe, *My Congenials*, Vol.1, p.233.

19. 'Memoirs', p.129.

20. Joy Hooton, *Stories of Herself When Young*, Chapter 11.

21. Ibid., p.289.

22. Ibid., p.291.

23. *My Brilliant Career*, p.166.

24. Hooton, p.292.

25. See Barnard, *Miles Franklin*, p.69.

26. *Cockatoos*, FP MSS445/8.

27. Norman Lindsay, *Bohemians of the Bulletin*, p.144.

28. SMF to JH, MEF and MES, 8/6/34, FP26.

29. Cited in Vivian Smith, ed., *Nettie Palmer*, p.26.

30. Red Page, *The Bulletin*, 17/11/54.

31. Colin Roderick's biography, *Miles Franklin*, is the most obvious example.

CHAPTER 12

181C HIGH STREET, KENSINGTON

1 . See Hermione Lee, *Virginia Woolf*, pp.473 and 742–3.

2 . Virginia Woolf, *Diary*, V.3, p.51.

3 . MEF to SMF, March 1934, FP16.

4 . MEF to SMF, 1/5/34, FP16.

5 . SMF to MEF, 22/4/44, FP120.

6 . *Moles*, p.49.

7 . SMF to MES, undated, 1936, FP25.

8 . SMF to MES, 22/6/45, FP25.

9 . SMF to MEF, 2/1/29, FP119.

10. Diary, 20/9/27, FP2.

11. SMF to MEF, 6/12/30, FP16.

12. SMF to MEF, 8/4/31, FP16.

13. MEF to sisters, 8/9/31, NLA.

14. Diary, 3/7/31, FP2.

15. MEF to SMF, 28/9/36, FP17.

16. Miles Franklin, Diary, 5/8/31, FP2.

17. Diary, 19/10/31, FP2.

18. Diary, 1/8/31, FP2.

19. SMF to MEF, 4/5/4-, FP120.

20. Diary, 3,4 & 7/5/32, FP2.
21. Diary, 2/11/31, FP2.
22. MEF to sisters, 17/11/31, NLA.
23. Cited in Roe, Vol.1, p.248.
24. D.J. Mulvaney, *Australian Dictionary of Biography*, 1891–1939, p.35.
25. P. Young collection, SLV, Box 23.
26. MEF to sisters, 26/10/27, NLA.
27. MEF to SMF, n.d., FP16.
28. Diary, 15/5/31, FP2.
29. R.R. Marett and T.K. Penniman, *Spencer's Last Journey*.
30. Diary, 1/12/31, FP2.
31. Diary, 25/6/32, FP2.
32. Diary, 6/8/32, FP2.
33. WS Diary, P.R. Stephensen Papers, ML MSS 1284, Box 124.
34. *Miles Franklin: A Tribute*, p.37.
35. ABC Radio, *The Coming Out Show*, 18 August 1979.
36. WS Diary, 3/7/32.
37. Diary, 16/7/32, FP2.
38. WS Diary, 16/7/32.
39. Ibid., 17/7/32.
40. Ibid., 19/7/32.
41. Ibid., 17/8/32.
42. Diary, 7/9/32, FP2.
43. MEF to sisters, 4/10/32, NLA.

CHAPTER 13

SECRETS

1. SMF to MEF, 11/4/29, FP119.
2. SMF to MEF, 26/3/35, FP17.
3. JH to SMF, 18/1/34, FP26.
4. SMF to JH, 13/7/34, FP26.
5. SMF to JH, 19/11/34, FP26.
6. JH to SMF, ?/11/33, FP26.
7. JH to SMF, 24/1/34, FP26.
8. SMF to JH, 19/11/34, FP26.
9. SMF to JH, 27/2/34, FP26.
10. MES to SMF, 5/4/34, FP25.
11. MES to SMF, 30/11/36, FP25.
12. SMF to MES, 8/1/40, FP25.
13. SMF to MES, 31/7/34, FP25.
14. JH to SMF, 19/4/34; 6/9/34, FP25.
15. Nigel Nicolson, *Portrait of a Marriage*, p.202.
16. JH to SMF, 31/10/34, FP26.
17. Diary, 12/6/33, FP2.
18. SMF to JH, 11/1/48, FP26.
19. SMF to JH, 10/8/49, FP26.
20. SMF to JH, 4/12/34, FP26.
21. SMF to MEF, 18/2/[33], FP16.
22. SMF to MEF, 22/1/34, FP16.
23. SMF to JH, 6/12/[33], FP26.
24. SMF to JH, 27/2/34, FP26.
25. JH to SMF, 12/7/34, FP26.
26. MEF to SMF, 29/10/28, FP16.
27. JH to SMF, n.d.[1933–34], FP26.
28. SMF to MEF, 27/3/34, FP16.
29. SMF to JH, 26/9/34, FP26.
30. SMF to MEF, 24/7/36, FP17.
31. MEF to SMF, 10/8/36, FP17.
32. SMF to MEF, 13/8/36, FP17.
33. Valerie Kent, 'Alias Miles Franklin', in C. Ferrier, ed., *Gender, Politics and Fiction*, p.57.
34. SMF to MEF, undated, FP120.
35. *Miles Franklin: A Tribute*, pp.35–36.
36. Barnard, *Miles Franklin*, p.3.
37. Ellis, *Studies*, Vol.3 (2nd edition), p.81.
38. SMF to MEF, 2/1/29, FP119.
39. SMF to MEF, 25/2/31, FP16.
40. Roe, 'Chivalry and Social Policy in the Antipodes', p.401.
41. SMF to MEF, 16/8/44, FP120.
42. Diary 1938–42, Moir Papers, SLV 12343, box 3131/1.
43. MEF to SMF, 28/9/40, FP17.
44. SMF to MEF, 21/11/40, FP119.
45. MEF to SMF, 19/2/43, FP18
46. MEF to SMF, 6/5/30, FP16.
47. Lasser, '"Let Us Be Sisters Forever"', p.168.
48. SMF to MES, 27/2/46, FP25.
49. Draft letter to Helen Heney, March 1954. Cited in Roe, *My Congenials*, Vol.2, p.343.

CHAPTER 14

'AN EXHILARATION OF TRAGEDY'

1. SMF to MEF, 29/10/34, FP16.
2. MEF to SMF, 13/2/33, FP16.
3. MEF to SMF, 5/12/34, FP16.
4. *Bark House Days*, ppvii–viii.
5. SMF to MEF, 7/4/35, FP17.
6. MEF to SMF, 26/5/36, FP17.
7. Virginia Moore, *The Life and Eager Death of Emily Brontë*. Commentary in *English Studies*, V.19, 1937, pp.28–31.
8. MEF to SMF, 16/9/36, FP17.
9. SMF to MEF, 8/10/36, FP17.
10. SMF to MEF, 20/3/37, FP17.
11. SMF to MEF, 13/4/36 (Content of letter indicates that it should be 1937), FP17.
12. MEF to SMF, May 1937, FP17.
13. MEF to SMF, 20/12/37, FP17.
14. *Moles*, p.50.
15. SMF to MEF, 2/8/43, FP120.
16. SMF to MEF, 14/7/37, FP17.
17. MEF to SMF, 2/8/37, FP17.
18. MEF to SMF, 18/8/37, FP17.
19. ABC Radio, *The Coming Out Show*, 18 August 1979.
20. SMF to MEF, 12/3/40, FP119.
21. MES to SMF, 30/11/36, FP25.
22. MEF to sisters, 13/4/37, NLA.
23. MEF to SMF, 7/5/39, FP17.
24. Diary, 28/8/39, SLV.
25. MES to SMF, 22/9/39, FP25.
26. Ibid.
27. JH to SMF, 7/7/44, FP26.
28. MEF to SMF, 11/4/41, FP18.
29. MES to SMF, 22/9/39, FP25.
30. MEF to SMF, 1/11/39, FP17.
31. SMF to MES, 8/1/40, FP25.
32. MES to SMF, 16/2/40, FP25.
33. MEF to sisters, March 1940, NLA.

34. MEF to SMF, 11/4/41, FP18.
35. 'Memoirs', p.122.
36. Moir Papers, SLV, MS12191, Box 2764/9.
37. SMF to MEF, 28/12/40, FP17.
38. Diary, 12/10/40.
39. JH to SMF, 7/7/44, FP26.
40. MES to SMF, 1/3/45, FP25.
41. MES to SMF, 26/6/44, FP25.
42. MEF to SMF, 21/9/44, FP19.
43. SMF to MEF, 1/4/45, FP120.
44. SMF to MES, 3/11/45, FP25.
45. MES to SMF, 2/1/46, FP25.
46. MES to SMF, 28/1/46, FP25.
47. SMF to EF, 27/2/46, FP21.
48. *The Wonder and the Apple*, p.30.

CHAPTER 15

POSTSCRIPT

1. MES to SMF, 6/5/46, FP25.
2. MES to SMF, 3/3/46, FP25.
3. SMF to EF, 17/4/46, FP21.
4. SMF to EF, 30/8/46, FP21.
5. EF to SMF, 8/9/46, FP21.
6. SMF to EF, 7/9/48, FP21.
7. JH to SMF, 26/7/49, FP26.
8. MES to SMF, 11/5/48, FP25.
9. SMF to MES, 22/12/49, FP25.
10. SMF to MES, 27/2/46, FP25.
11. SMF to MES, 3/9/46, FP25.
12. MES to SMF, 22/10/46, FP25.
13. MES to SMF, 24/2/52, FP25.
14. MES to SMF, 30/4/50, FP25.
15. SMF to MES, 29/5/50, FP25.
16. EF to J.K. Moir, 9/4/52, Moir Papers, SLV Box 78/6.
17. MES to SMF, 24/4/46, FP25.
18. SMF to MES, 8/4/46, FP25.
19. MES to SMF, 24/2/52, FP25.

PRIMARY SOURCES

MANUSCRIPTS

Franklin Papers, Mitchell Library, MSS364: 2–3, 16–19, 25, 26, 119–120; MSS1360.
Fullerton Papers, Mitchell Library, MSS 2342: 2,10.
Fullerton Papers, National Library of Australia, MS6608.
Moir Papers, State Library of Victoria (La Trobe Collection).
Stephensen Papers. Mitchell Library.
Goldstein Papers, Fawcett Library, City of London Polytechnic.
Pitt Papers, State Library of Victoria (La Trobe Collection).
P. Young Collection, State Library of Victoria.

PUBLICATIONS: MARY FULLERTON

Moods and Melodies, Endacott, Melbourne, 1908.
The Australian Comic Dictionary of Words, by Turner O'Lingo, E.J. Cole, Melbourne, 1916.
The Breaking Furrow, Endacott, Melbourne, 1921.
Bark House Days, Endacott, Melbourne, 1921.
Two Women: Clare: Margaret, by Two Anonymous Writers, Philpot, London, 1923.
The People of the Timber Belt, Philpot, London, 1925.
The Australian Bush, Dent, 'Outward Bound Library' series, London, 1928.
A Juno of the Bush, Heath Cranton, London, 1930.
Bark House Days (illustrated edition, with 18 pen and ink sketches by Margaret Janes), Heath Cranton, London, 1931.
Rufus Sterne, by Robert Gray, Blackwood, Edinburgh, 1932.
The Murders at the Crabapple Cafe, by Gordon Manners, Jenkins, London, 1933.
Moles Do So Little With Their Privacy, by 'E', Angus & Robertson, Sydney, 1942.
The Wonder and the Apple: More Poems by 'E', Angus & Robertson, Sydney, 1946.
Bark House Days, Melbourne University Press, Carlton, 1964.

SELECTED PUBLICATIONS: MILES FRANKLIN

My Brilliant Career, Blackwood, Edinburgh, 1901.
Some Everyday Folk and Dawn, Blackwood, Edinburgh, 1909.
The Net of Circumstance, by Mr and Mrs Ogniblat L'Artsau, Mills & Boon, London, 1915.

Up the Country, by Brent of Bin Bin, Blackwood, Edinburgh, 1928.

Ten Creek's Run, by Brent of Bin Bin, Blackwood, Edinburgh, 1930.

Old Blastus of Bandicoot, Palmer, London, 1931.

Back to Bool Bool, by Brent of Bin Bin, Blackwood, Edinburgh, 1931.

Bring The Monkey, Endeavour Press, Sydney, 1933.

All That Swagger, The Bulletin, Sydney, 1936.

Pioneers on Parade (with Dymphna Cusack), Angus & Robertson, Sydney, 1939.

Joseph Furphy (with Kate Baker), Angus & Robertson, Sydney, 1940.

My Career Goes Bung, Georgian House, Melbourne, 1946.

Prelude to Waking, by Brent of Bin Bin, Angus & Robertson, Sydney, 1950.

Cockatoos, by Brent of Bin Bin, Angus & Robertson, Sydney, 1954.

Gentlemen at Gyang Gyang, by Brent of Bin Bin, Angus & Robertson, Sydney, 1956.

Laughter, Not For a Cage, Angus & Robertson, Sydney, 1956.

Childhood at Brindabella, Angus & Robertson, Sydney, 1963.

On Dearborn Street, University of Queensland Press, St Lucia, 1981.

Bring the Monkey, Introduction by Bronwen Levy, Pandora, London and New York, 1987.

My Brilliant Career; My Career Goes Bung, Introduction by Elizabeth Webby, Collins/Angus & Robertson, Sydney, 1990.

SECONDARY SOURCES

Allen, Judith A., *Rose Scott: Vision and Revision in Feminism*, Oxford University Press, Melbourne, 1994.

Barnard, Marjorie, *Miles Franklin: The Story of a Famous Australian*, 1967, University of Queensland Press, St. Lucia, 1988.

Bomford, Janette M., *That Dangerous and Persuasive Woman: Vida Goldstein*, Melbourne University Press, 1993.

Brittain, Vera, *Radclyffe Hall: A Case of Obscenity?*, London, Femina, 1968.

Carpenter, Edward, *Love's-Coming-of-Age*, 1896, in Noel Greig (ed.), *Edward Carpenter: Selected Writings. Volume 1: Sex*.

———, *The Intermediate Sex*, Allen & Unwin, London, 1908.

———, *Towards Democracy*, Allen & Unwin, London, 1915.

Claus, Ruth F., 'Confronting Homosexuality: A Letter from Frances Wilder', *Signs*, 2:4,1977, pp.928–933.

Coleman, Verna, *Miles Franklin in America: Her Unknown (Brilliant) Career*, Angus & Robertson, London, 1981.

de Lauretis, Teresa, *The Practice of Love: Lesbian Sexuality and Perverse Desire*, Indiana University Press, Bloomington and Indianapolis, 1994.

Ellis, Henry Havelock, *Studies in the Psychology of Sex, Vol. II, Sexual Inversion*, F. A. Davis, Philadelphia, 1922. First published in London as Vol. 1, 1897.

———, 'Fiction in the Australian Bush', in *Views and Reviews: A Selection of Uncollected Articles 1884–1932*, Houghton Mifflin, Boston and New

York, 1932. First published in the English magazine, *Weekly Critical Review*, 17 September, 1903.

Emerson, Ralph Waldo, *Essays*, Routledge & Sons, London and New York, 1886.

Faderman, Lillian, *Surpassing The Love of Men: Romantic Friendship and Love Between Women from the Renaissance to the Present*, The Women's Press, London, 1985.

Franklin, Miles, 'Rose Scott: Some Aspects of her Personality and Work', in Eldershaw, Flora (ed.), *The Peaceful Army*, 1938. New edition by Dale Spender, Penguin, Ringwood, 1988.

Gowland, Pat, 'The Women's Peace Army', in Windschuttle, Elizabeth (ed.), *Women, Class and History: Feminist Perspectives on Australia 1788–1978*. Fontana, Melbourne, 1980.

Greig, Noel (ed.), *Edward Carpenter: Selected Writings. Volume 1: Sex*, GMP Publishers, London, 1984.

Hicks, Neville, *'This Sin and Scandal': Australia's Population Debate 1891–1911*, Australian National University Press, Canberra, 1978.

Hooton, Joy, *Stories of Herself When Young: Autobiographies of Childhood by Australian Women*, Oxford University Press, Melbourne, 1990.

Kelly, Farley, 'The "Woman Question" in Melbourne 1880–1914', PhD thesis, Monash University, Melbourne, 1983.

———, 'Vida Goldstein: Political Woman', in Marilyn Lake and Farley Kelly (eds.), *Double Time: Women in Victoria – 150 Years*, Penguin, Ringwood, 1985.

Kent, Valerie, 'Alias Miles Franklin', in Carole Ferrier (ed.), *Gender, Politics and Fiction*, University of Queensland Press, St. Lucia, 1985.

Kirkby, Diane, *Alice Henry: The Power of Pen and Voice*, Cambridge University Press, Cambridge, 1991.

Lasser, Carol, '"Let us be Sisters Forever": The Sororal Model of Nineteenth-Century Female Friendship', *Signs*, vol. 14, no. 1, 1988.

Lee, Hermione, *Virginia Woolf*, Chatto & Windus, London, 1996.

Lindsay, Norman, *Bohemians of the Bulletin*, Angus & Robertson, Sydney, 1965.

Little, Graham, *Friendship: Being Ourselves With Others*, Text, Melbourne, 1993.

Manson, Cecil and Celia, *Doctor Agnes Bennett*, Michael Joseph, London, 1960.

Marett, R.R. and T.K. Penniman (eds.), *Spencer's Last Journey*, Clarendon Press, Oxford, 1931.

Marlatt, Daphne, 'Self-representation and Fictionalysis', *Tessera*, vol. 8, Spring 1990.

Miles Franklin: a Tribute, Bread and Cheese Club, Melbourne, 1955.

Modjeska, Drusilla, *Exiles at Home: Australian Women Writers 1925–1945*, Angus & Robertson, Sydney, 1981.

Moore, Virginia, *The Life and Eager Death of Emily Brontë*, Rich & Cowan, London, 1936.

Mulvaney, D.J., Sir Walter Baldwin Spencer, in *Australian Dictionary of Biography*, 1891–1939, Melbourne University Press, Carlton.

—————, and J.H. Calaby, *'So Much That Is New': Baldwin Spencer, 1860–1929*, Melbourne University Press, Carlton, 1985.

Nicolson, Nigel, *Portrait of a Marriage*, Macdonald Futura, London, 1974.

Parker, Andrew, Mary Russo, Doris Sommer and Patricia Yaeger (eds.), *Nationalisms and Sexualities*, Routledge, New York and London, 1992.

Raitt, Suzanne, *Vita and Virginia: The Work and Friendship of V. Sackville-West and Virginia Woolf*, Clarendon Press, Oxford, 1993.

Rich, Adrienne, 'Compulsory Heterosexuality and Lesbian Existence', *Signs*, vol. 5, no. 4, 1980.

Roderick, Colin, *Miles Franklin: Her Brilliant Career*, Rigby, Adelaide, 1982.

Roe, Jill, 'The Significant Silence: Miles Franklin's Middle Years', *Meanjin*, V39, 1980.

—————, 'Chivalry and Social Policy in the Antipodes', *Historical Studies*, vol. 22, no. 88, April 1987.

—————, (ed.), *My Congenials: Miles Franklin and Friends in Letters*, 2 vols, Angus & Robertson, Sydney, 1993.

Rose, June, *Marie Stopes and the Sexual Revolution*, Faber & Faber, London and Boston, 1993.

Sedgewick, Eve Kosofsky, *The Epistemology of the Closet*, University of California Press, Berkeley, 1990.

Showalter, Elaine, *Sexual Anarchy: Gender and Culture at the Fin de Siècle*, Virago, London, 1991.

Smith, Vivian (ed.), *Nettie Palmer*, University of Queensland Press, St. Lucia, 1988.

Smith-Rosenberg, Carroll, 'The Female World of Love and Ritual: Relations Between Women in Nineteenth-Century America', *Signs*, vol. 1, no. 1, 1975.

Souhami, Diana, *Gluck: her biography*, Pandora, London, 1988.

—————, *Gertrude and Alice*, Pandora, London, 1991.

Stanley, Liz and Ann Morley, *The Life and Death of Emily Wilding Davison*, The Women's Press, London, 1988.

Stanley, Liz, 'Romantic Friendship? Some Issues in Researching Lesbian History and Biography', *Women's History Review*, vol. 1, no. 2, 1992.

Thompson, Tierl (ed.), *Dear Girl: The diaries and letters of two working women 1897–1917*, The Women's Press, London, 1987.

Vicinus, Martha, *Independent Women: Women, Work and Community for Single Women, 1850–1920*, Virago, London, 1985.

Watson, Don, *Caledonia Australis*, Vintage, Sydney, 1997.

Whitelaw, Lis, *The Life and Rebellious Times of Cicely Hamilton*, The Women's Press, London, 1990.

Woolf, Virginia, *The Diary*, vol. 2. 1920–1924, Anne Olivier Bell (ed.), The Hogarth Press, London, 1978.

—————, *The Diary*, vol. 3. 1925–1930, Anne Olivier Bell (ed.), The Hogarth Press, London, 1980.

Onlywomen Press books are available from libraries and bookshops throughout the United Kingdom, Europe, Australia and North America.

For a free mail-order catalogue, write to:

Onlywomen Press
Department FC
40d St Lawrence Terrace
London W10 5ST